Association for M
Level Education
Westerville, Ohio

Advisory

Finding the Best Fit
for Your school

James B. Burns
Jaynellen Behre Jenkins
J. Thomas Kane

Printed in the United States of America.

ISBN: 978-1-56090-243-0

Library of Congress Cataloging-in-Publication Data

Burns, James B.

  Advisory : finding the best fit for your school / James B. Burns, Jaynellen Behre Jenkins, J. Thomas Kane.

    p. cm.

  Includes bibliographical references and index.

  ISBN 978-1-56090-243-0 (alk. paper)

  1. Middle schools--United States--Administration. 2. Advisory boards--United States. I. Jenkins, Jaynellen Behre. II. Kane, J. Thomas. III. Title.

  LB2822.2.B875 2011

  373.236--dc23

                          2011026327

AMLE.

Association for Middle Level Education
formerly National Middle School Association

We're for young adolescents
     For ever-evolving teens
     For curious, questioning youngsters
     For many mood swings
     For multiple-sized young teens

We're for young adolescents
     Experiencing solid challenging classes
     Exploring interdisciplinary adventures
     Experiencing caring advisory activities
     Being cared for by a dedicated staff

We're for young adolescents
     Living healthy lives
     Contributing to community service
     Developing positive personalities
     Adding to a caring school community

We're for young adolescents
being all they can be in
middle school

We're for young adolescents!

Tom Kane

Acknowledgements

As is always the case when a book is published, a great many people have directly and indirectly contributed to this work. In our case, many people deserve recognition and thanks, such as the principals and teachers who completed the survey instrument that provided data to inform our discussions and members of New Mexico Highlands University and New Mexico Middle Level Educators whose organizations supported this research.

There are also a good many persons that can be named who made specific contributions and we want to express our gratitude to the following:

        Michel Tenorio
        Daniel Maestas
        Ronald Murray
        Veronica Torres
        Todd Wynward
        Ross Burkhardt
        J'Ann Wright
        Carol Smith
        Dave Braun y Harycki
        Chris Stevenson
        James Barnes

And finally we offer our thanks and appreciation to John Lounsbury and Carla Weiland, editors and members of the Publications Team at the Association for Middle Level Education, for their assistance in bringing this work to fruition.

Contents

1

What Is Advisory?

"Advisory" lacks a clear meaning. When offering an opinion on any aspect of an advisory program, one almost always has to preface the statement with "It all depends." For instance, when considering the basic question "How large should an advisory group be?" a response has to note that it all depends. For instance: will the group include students that the advisor teaches? Will the group stay together for more than one year? Will they meet daily or twice a month? among other considerations. The stock answer of "12-15 advisees" just can't be universal; it all depends. Also, what is seen as an advantage for one arrangement, such as not teaching any of one's advisees, is considered a disadvantage when viewed from a different perspective. It all depends...

—John Lounsbury

How, then, shall we start this book? Tom suggested we launch it by sharing our thoughts about what advisory is and offered these statements:

> Advisory is an essential and integral part of a developmentally responsive middle school. One that fosters trust, communication, and a true sense of belonging for the student as the result of positive relationships between students and teachers, and students and fellow students.

> Advisory is a vehicle to enhance the essential relational work within the middle school community so no pupil is lost amid the school population.

> Advisory is an opportunity for discussion and dialogue on issues important to young adolescents. It enhances positive self-concepts and gives pupils direction toward positive lives as young teens.

Jaynellen added these statements:

> Advisory in middle schools ensures that each young adolescent learner will be known well by at least one caring adult at school. Advisory is intended to scaffold each student's likelihood for success in school, including academic achievement, with a distinct focus on development of positive relationships and effective communication with both peers and adults.

Finally, Jim Burns brought the initial discussion to a close with this one-liner: *Advisory is not a curriculum but a relationship.*

These "definitions" make it clear that the term "advisory" is indeed a broad and nebulous term that is not easily fully encapsulated in a sentence or two. While an advisory program is usually the major element in a middle school's efforts to fulfill its advocacy responsibility, the exact nature of that element varies tremendously. But what always distinguishes advisory from content courses of study is that it is primarily relational work with a focus on the affective aspects of an education. However, it should be said— and emphasized— that advisory supports and serves both directly and indirectly the cognitive, academic side of an education.

Advisory's prominence in the middle school movement

Those who envisioned something different and better than traditional junior high schools for the education of young adolescents quickly made teacher-based guidance or advisory a key element in the newly proposed middle school. In 1982, the recently established National Middle School Association (NMSA, now AMLE) published a position paper, entitled simply *This We Believe*. It identified ten essential elements of a "true" middle school. One was "comprehensive advising and counseling," described as follows:

> Homebase or advisor programs which provide individuals with regular opportunities for interaction with a small group of peers and a caring adult…. These programs involve regularly scheduled meetings which offer opportunities for interaction that lead to increased self-awareness, the consideration of values, and the development of understandings needed to deal with various school, home, or peer-related problems. (pp. 18–19)

In the late 1980s, amidst growing support for middle level education, the influential publication *Turning Points: Preparing America's Youth for the 21st Century* (1989) was published by the Council on Adolescent Development of the Carnegie Corporation of New York. It, too, called for creating small communities for learning and identified as a key element of such communities "small group advisories that ensure that every student is known well by at least one adult" (p. 9). NMSA expanded upon its founding position paper in *This We Believe: Developmentally Responsive Middle Level Schools* (1995). In this re-visioning, advisory was included among six key characteristics of a middle level school in asserting the need for individual students "to have an understanding adult as an advocate and guide." Teacher advocates, advisory programs, and homebase are named explicitly as providing "opportunities for advocates to meet regularly with students in small groups" (p. 31).

With the advent of No Child Left Behind (2002), intensified emphasis on accountability within separate subjects and standardized test performance worked against advisory. NMSA responded with a third edition, *This We Believe: Successful Schools for Young Adolescents* (2003). In this version, the adult advocate for every student recommendation included elaboration of the adviser's specific role.

In *Turning Points 2000: Educating Adolescents in the 21st Century* (Jackson & Davis, 2000), advocacy and advisory were discussed at some length as crucial aspects of an effective middle grades school. In a 2005 publication, *This We Believe in Action: Implementing Successful Middle Schools* (NMSA), both advocacy and advisory were endorsed and thoroughly described in the chapter "An Adult Advocate for Every Student" (pp. 63–75). In 2008, the National Association of Secondary School Principals issued a major report, *Breaking Ranks in the Middle: Strategies for Leading Middle Level Reform*. One of nine cornerstone strategies advanced in this document is "Implement a comprehensive advisory or other program that ensures that each student has frequent and meaningful opportunities to meet with an adult to plan and assess the student's academic, personal, and social development" (p. 8).

Then, most recently, NMSA published a fourth edition of its position paper, *This We Believe: Keys to Educating Young Adolescents* (2010). Intentionally departing from the "limitations of high-stakes-testing-only reform" (pp. 43–44), this edition articulated 16 characteristics of the successful middle grades school. Addressed under the heading of advocacy, advisory is described as "when students and their advisors meet regularly during the school day," and a program that "helps students develop respect for self and others; compassion; a workable set of values; and the skills of cooperation, decision making, and goal setting" (p. 35).

Thus, advisory has prevailed for more than 30 years in policy positions as an essential, recommended component of a middle school. It has endured, we believe, in spite of whatever difficulties it has encountered in becoming operational because it serves a genuine need, one no other middle level component addresses to ensure that every student is well known, that everybody is somebody, and that each student has a voice in his or her school life. Indicative of its recognized importance, along the way advisory has been pegged as the linchpin of the middle school movement and as the soul of the middle school. Chris Stevenson, master teacher and noted author, claims that teacher advisory is the very best idea in the middle level movement!

Grounding advisory in school leadership

This is a book for school leaders—for those who seek to lead or be active in an effort to design or refine relational experiences for young adolescents and for those directly involved as advisors. In addition, anyone desiring to understand the how and why of advisory will find this resource particularly helpful. Do not confuse our use of the term "leader;" our meaning of leader is not reserved for principals or administrators. For example, all three authors are educational leaders, but only one, Jaynellen, is an active middle school principal. Tom served for many years as a principal but has gained considerable experience in recent years as a consultant. Jim, now a professor of educational leadership, was a middle grades exceptional education teacher for 19 years. So we wrote this book for people just like ourselves, school leaders with varying backgrounds but all committed to carrying out programs that will result in a better education for young adolescents.

Believing in full disclosure, we begin with a confession: there is little new here. The ideas in this volume have been around for decades, but the lack of originality may be a virtue—everything suggested has been proven in practice.

Although this is not a book of theory, it has a solid theoretical underpinning. The book is based on materials in the literature, our collective and extensive experiences, a status survey we conducted, and specific observations and reports of what schools in the United States and elsewhere actually do in advisory programs. The ideas are solid—tried and true. We present many faces and facets of advisory. You will need to consider thoroughly all possibilities in order to judge what might work best in your school, be it a traditional public school—if there is such a thing—an alternative or charter school, a private prep school, or a parochial school—remember, it all depends.

How this book is organized and should be used

This opening chapter introduces the concept of advisory. Your understanding will evolve as you work through the chapters and consider all the organizational and curricular possibilities of advisory.

Don't bypass Chapter 2, "Why Advisory?" assuming that everybody in middle school knows why advisory is necessary. This chapter supplies a meaningful context and a readiness for your study of the nuts, bolts, and nuances of advisory. We discuss the critical matter of selecting the aims or goals for advisory and offer a process a faculty can use to determine their program's major goals. In conclusion, we describe the status study we used to gather data to inform our writing.

Chapter 3 provides a wide-ranging presentation of what might comprise curriculum in advisories with many examples from schools. Advisory programs initially involved dividing up the students in each grade into small groups, providing a period in the schedule for the groups to meet, and assigning an advisor to each small group. The almost endless variations of this basic arrangement are discussed in Chapter 4, "Organizational Considerations: How Many, How Often, How Long, Who." In this chapter we detail variations in group size, length of period, frequency of meetings, scheduling, and related matters that, when resolved, give a program its distinctiveness.

Chapter 5 considers the increasingly popular multiyear arrangements that are particularly well-suited to carry out advisory and advocacy responsibilities. In Chapter 6 we discuss the tangential but critical matters of preparation and professional development for advisors and ways to assess and evaluate a program. A brief seventh chapter concludes the book with some thoughts to consider and a challenge.

Our intent, we repeat, is to fully inform readers on all aspects of advisory programs so that readers who are considering starting an advisory program or reviving a stalled one will be aware of all the ins and outs of advisory, the pros and cons of varying arrangements, the need to recognize the interrelatedness of elements and ultimately find the strategy or approach that would fit their particular situations. We do not make specific recommendations for the best approach; that is your decision after you have considered all the presented possibilities in light of your school's culture. We do, however, sincerely believe middle level leaders in schools without a viable program must take the initiative and establish an advisory program that is so essential to providing the full education young adolescents need and deserve. The time is now!

2
Why Advisory?

It had been my bias that kids drop out because they are not doing well academically. However, when you talk to dropouts, one of the reasons they drop out is that nobody knows them. They say, "Who cares if I am here or not? No one would even notice if I don't come to school." And so the idea of being known, noticed, and cared about in a place as a reason to stay there very much resonated with me.

—Sarah Brody Shulkind (2008)

Well, she's no one's girl
And she winds a finger up through her curls
Tries to see out through the world of school

She does not take her lecture notes
Sits in her desk and tries to cope
She's got no friends and she's got no hope and it's cruel

And there's no one at home
She spends the endless hours alone
And she's not allowed to telephone
The friends she does not have
And she cannot understand….

—Lyrics by Monte Selby
"She's No One's Girl"

During the 2008 National Middle School Association Annual Conference in Denver, as the authors tried to exit the Hyatt Regency following a presentation of our recent advisory research, we wound through the throng of conferees who were equally busy coming, going, or simply congregating, when we heard someone call out our names. "Jim, Tom, Jaynellen!" We turned toward the voice to see John Lounsbury gesturing to us through the gathered mass. Weaving and dodging through the crowd, we reached our friend to greet and shake the hand of this veteran leader. As we reached him, he spoke in a somewhat hushed tone four words: "Advisory is rising again."

The meaning of this statement was, to us, a very big deal. On a certain level—the most obvious one—John was speaking of an impending resurgence of the middle school philosophy that features advisory. The middle school concept, he believed, would rise like a phoenix from the ashes following nearly a decade of stagnation, if not regression. The NMSA conferees in Denver that week were acutely aware of standing on the cusp of a presidential election of historic proportions. In less than a week America would elect a new leader. The air was charged with the promise of change. It was palpable.

Although the anticipated change in federal educational policies didn't occur as immediately as hoped, there were already enough signs appearing in the professional literature and elsewhere to indicate that change was, indeed, coming. Dissatisfaction with No Child Left Behind was prominently and publically voiced. Organizations and well-respected leaders were calling for an emphasis on creativity, collaboration, teaming, small learning communities, and other practices which the middle school concept had always included. The goal of making adequate yearly progress, whether met or not, no longer was seen as a goal worth pursuing or was able to inspire educators who genuinely cared about kids and wanted to provide a holistic education for all. As Tom Sergiovanni (2006) observed: "Effectiveness" has become the new low bar by which schools are assessed. (Effectiveness is associated closely with current icons of adequacy and proficiency.) He noted that effective schools may succeed operationally, in congeniality, and even with instructional leadership, but they fail to achieve the ascendant levels of professionalism, collegiality, and community—the places where true excellence resides. In the end, the relational work embedded in advisory is often the distinguishing factor in high performing middle schools that separates them from thousands of other middle schools presumably striving toward excellence but unable to reach it. Establishing meaningful connections through relationships is fundamental for achieving what Peter Senge (1994) referred to as the "higher-hanging fruit" and what John Dewey saw as a seamless fusion between living and learning. Advisory, then, is critical to achieving that fulfilling educational experience every young adolescent needs and deserves.

Middle level educators who pursue advisory as an investment toward fulfilling greater needs will find this work to be among the most gratifying and fulfilling aspects of teaching young adolescents that former NMSA President Ross Burkhardt called "the most important work on the planet."

Review: Why advisory?

To those who understand the notion that every instructional coin has two sides––transmission of skills and knowledge on the one side and establishing rapport with learners on the other—the benefit of relational investment with learners is abundantly clear. However, for those few teachers exclusively focused on utilizing every instructional minute to cover material, investing any time in advisory seems a sellout. Therefore, a first step in preparing middle grades teachers for advisory responsibility requires that all have developed a genuine common belief in and a commitment to advisory.

In her study that culminated in an award-winning dissertation on advisory, Sarah Brody Shulkind (2007) discovered that high school dropouts identified anonymity as a major reason they decided to leave school. "The idea of being known, noticed, and cared about in a place as a reason to stay" resonated with her—as it had with us. As middle level educators know full well, middle schoolers are even more likely to feel like "lost" children. The few poignant words from Monte Selby's song "She's No One's Girl (1997) that we opened the chapter with, capture this all-too-common situation among young adolescents. We are reminded, too, of Richard Lipka's (1997) pithy statement: "Cognitive learning is hard-won by someone whose life is in affective disarray!" (p. 31)

When we help schools undertake advisory, we often begin with a story from an Idaho educator, Jean Mizer. Her true account *Cipher in the Snow* (1964) tells about a high school student, Cliff Evans, who dies on the way to school and the subsequent discovery that no one in the school really knew him or anything about him. This story has been in print for more than 50 years. In fact, most educators who have been in the middle grades for a couple of decades or more have either read the piece or seen it dramatized in a short NEA film produced by Brigham Young University.

We find Mizer's narrative, which takes just over six minutes to read aloud, an extremely powerful way to focus a group of educators on the critical value and importance of establishing relationships within schools. Although the story's setting is a ranching community in southeast Idaho, we have seen its telling visibly move educators in an inner-city school in Newark, New Jersey, and elsewhere. Its message is universal. Cipher ends with these statements:

> We couldn't find ten students in the school who had known Cliff well enough to attend the funeral as his friends. So the student body officers and a committee from the junior class went as a group to the church, being politely sad. I attended the services with them, and sat through it with a lump of cold lead in my chest and a big resolve growing through me.
>
> I've never forgotten Cliff Evans nor that resolve. He has been my challenge year after year, class after class. I look for veiled eyes or bodies scrounged into a seat in an alien world. "Look, kids," I say silently. "I may not do anything else for you this year, but not one of you is going to come out of here as a nobody. I'll work or fight to the bitter end doing battle with society and the school board, but I won't have one of you coming out of there thinking himself a zero."
>
> Most of the time—not always, but most of the time—I've succeeded. (p. 10)

Always, you could hear a pin drop as those final words, "I've succeeded," are spoken. There are many other real-life stories that highlight the critical importance and potential impact of establishing genuine relationships with students. "Three Letters from Teddy," published as *The Bracelet* (2003) by Elizabeth Ballard, is an example that has been widely shared. And, indeed, when most middle level educators stop to think about it, they recall an incident in which a teacher who cared "saved" a student.

Establishing specific goals for advisory

Rarely will you, as a school leader (whether a teacher, counselor, or administrator), lead a charge toward advisory with a group that is fully ready and invested in moving ahead. But when you do get a group to that point, it is natural for the members to want to charge full speed ahead and set up the programmatic structure. After all, why reinvent the wheel?

While we do encourage you to beg, borrow, and steal ideas that work well, we also know that one of the biggest mistakes in establishing advisory is to accept a hand-me-down program or simply to buy one of the published advisory curriculums. Perhaps the most important choice to make when constructing an advisory program is that of selecting appropriate purposes or aims. Regardless of the other programmatic decisions—grouping, scheduling, themes—no decision will have greater impact on the success of advisory than the selection of overarching aims that guide the specific planning and conduct of the program.

So, take time to develop a clearly stated list of purposes and aims that is fully endorsed by all. Some lofty philosophical statement? No! A long list of every affective concern that would be applicable? No! Rather, we suggest selecting three to five aims or goals that distinguish advisory from the regular curriculum and clearly separate advisory from any involvement in special intervention calling for a counselor or social worker. The following purposes provide an example:

Figure 2.1

> ## Purposes of Our Advisory Program
>
> 1. To ensure that every student is known well by at least one adult in the school
>
> 2. To ensure that students have time and opportunity to develop constructive friendships with other students
>
> 3. To help develop and support each student's expectations for success in school
>
> 4. To uncover and explore each student's personal interests in regard to learning and to life out of school
>
> 5. To give each student a voice as an active participant among a community of learners

Why these out of the numerous social, psychological, cognitive, somatic, or even spiritual possibilities? First, we intentionally limited the list to five. This decision was not arbitrary. Cognitive researcher Irving Sato tells us that humans easily recall (and can therefore activate) three to five ideas from a list. So, while it might seem sensible to have a dozen desirable purposes, if students, teachers, and parents can't quickly call up these collective purposes, the program will lack impact. According to Galassi, Gulledge, and Cox in their book *Advisory: Definitions, Descriptions, Decisions and Directions* (1998), "The purposes that advisory may serve are so numerous that the biggest task may be to identify a primary need or manageable cluster of needs to be met by the program" (p. 27). In terms of program focus, less can truly be more.

We like the aims we suggested in part because they are derived from a research study. Many years ago, New England League of Middle Schools' director Jim Garvin (1987) surveyed more than a thousand parents of students in the middle grades, asking what they wanted for their youngsters from the middle school. The following is a summary, in priority order, of the parents' collective expectations:

1. When my child goes to school, more than anything else I want to know that he/she is safe.

2. I want to know that when my child is in school, he/she knows at least one adult well enough to go to when support is needed.

3. I want to know that the school is concerned about helping my youngster develop constructive friendships.

4. I expect that the school will provide my youngster with opportunities to get involved in activities.

5. When my youngster comes home from school, I want to know that he/she has had enough good experiences to want to return the next day.

6. While my child is in middle school, I want to know that the school is teaching him/her what he/she will need to be prepared for high school. (pp. 3–4)

After first wanting a safe school, the parents' collective priorities parallel those of our first three advisory aims. The fourth and fifth items follow Sergiovanni's call to stretch beyond proficiency toward Dewey's melding of "living and learning."

How best to go about selecting advisory purposes for your site? One way to gather data necessary for making this determination is to individually interview each faculty member, but a well-designed survey that provides a pencil-and-paper equivalent of an interview is more effective. It allows much the same data to be collected in a fraction of the time and in a form that easily can be consolidated. It is also superior to person-to-person interviewing in that colleagues can answer in a candid and confidential manner. An example of such a survey follows.

Figure 2.2

Advisory Focus Survey (to be completed anonymously)

1. Indicate the areas in which our students have the greatest needs that might be met in an advisory program. Rank your top five choices numerically. Check any additional choices, but do not numerically rank.

_____ community building	_____ school service
_____ developing responsibility	_____ team spirit
_____ organizational skills	_____ school government
_____ service to community	_____ personal interests
_____ constructive friendships	_____ bullying
_____ academic monitoring	_____ learning styles
_____ recognition of progress	_____ appreciating diversity
_____ high school readiness	_____ celebrations
_____ democratic participation	_____ student voice

2. List other areas where you think advisory should provide learning/leadership opportunities or support.

3. Are there specific areas you think advisory should intentionally avoid? Why?

4. Do you have past experience with advisory?

5. Would you help review results from this survey and develop the list of most preferred purposes or aims for advisory?

6. Would you be interested in participating in an advisory study/planning group? If, yes, please contact _____.

7. Other input:

A weighted review

Once surveys have been tallied, you will have a relatively long list of potential advisory purposes. Organize that list with the most-cited items clustered at the top, followed by less-cited items, and finally with least-cited items at the bottom.

Next, present the list at a meeting of the full faculty. Using large newsprint sheets, post on the walls around the room all the suggestions, on as many sheets as needed with lettering large enough to be read anywhere in the classroom. Issue five stick-on dots to each faculty member, explaining that they may distribute the dots as they see fit. For example, all five "votes" could be attached to one goal, or they could be distributed one-each to five items they see as most important, or any combination in between. Then let faculty members vote by walking around and casting their votes as they see fit. Use these weighted votes to identify the most preferred purposes. Once identified, these items will likely need to be further clarified and possibly consolidated by a steering committee, one on which any faculty member is invited to participate.

In addition, we suggest identifying one of the five goals for a special annual advisory focus. An advisory committee would select this focus to reflect a specific hot issue, such as cyber-bullying. This particular focus can be used for a semester or longer, but it should not automatically extend beyond that academic year. This focus should not, by any means, be the basis for all activities in that period. Periodically, the faculty should reconsider the goals, and possibly a new focus.

Careful selection of advisory purposes or aims is critical to the long-term success of a program. Aims should be brief enough to be memorable, yet clear enough so that advisors will be able to create activities to pursue them. Even though an aim is simply and clearly stated, it likely encompasses many sub-aims, so don't mistake a short list with a lack of depth. A brief list of aims need not limit possibilities for meaningful advisory activities. For example, our previously listed aim "To uncover and explore each student's personal interests in regard both to learning and to life outside school" could be narrowly interpreted and dealt with simply by surveying each student's hobbies or interests. But broadly considered, students' interests can lead to an array of relational advisory activities or career related curriculum-based projects.

An example of how a limited number of aims can provide rich activities is provided by Pacific Cascade Middle School in Issaquash, WA. Principal Dana Bailey reports that when her school initiated their advisory program called Lynx Life, they spent a great deal of time researching and studying to develop a sound, curriculum-based, structured program. Though they settled on just three main aims or goals, they developed sub-aims of specific student behaviors that would be achieved under each goal, as shown below.

Goal 1: Relationships

- Students will be known well by at least one adult in the building.

- Students will be supported by their advisors, who can act as liaisons.

- Students' sensitivity on issues of diversity and culture will increase.

- Students will feel a greater sense of school connectedness by becoming involved.

Goal 2: Navigate through academic future

- Students will understand the importance of planning for their academic futures.

- Students will support registration, and credit and graduation requirements.

- Students will learn effective study, organization, and time management skills.

- Advisors will help ensure all students are supported academically.

- Students will be exposed to a myriad of career choices and interests.

Goal 3: Leadership and decision-making skills

- Lynx Life will provide authentic opportunities to build leadership in every student.

- Advisors will teach and model effective decisions.

- Students will learn about social choices, consequences, and conflict resolution.

- Lynx Life will provide practice in dealing with peer pressure.

- Students will practice public speaking and listening skills.

—D. Bailey (personal communication, May 24, 2011)

Collaborative development is key to the success of even the most precise, memorable list of advisory aims. The discussions involved in the development of a list are most important in achieving the common commitment. Using some other school's well-worded goals just will not work because somebody else's choices will not resonate with your advisors. Authenticity of purpose matters most. A good list of aims will keep the program on course, with adjustments made from year-to-year as experience indicates.

Relevant research studies

The literature reveals few comprehensive studies on advisory programs, although many testimonials about successful programs have appeared in journals, and advisory was a part of many research studies that assessed a school's total efforts. A substantial number of doctoral dissertations on advisory have been conducted over the last decade that have been supportive and positive in their findings. One early research study by Putbrese (1989) examined student perceptions of advisory programs. The survey was distributed to a person in each state determined to have middle level expertise. That individual was directed to select two middle grades schools in that state that had advisory programs and two that did not and "to secure involvement from school officials in those four schools to participate in the survey" (p. 111). Each of the school leaders was asked to administer the survey to 50 seventh graders in the school. The study obtained approximately 3,400 completed surveys from a broad geographic distribution across the United States. The data compared perceptions on various issues or beliefs of student who had an advisory program with those of students who did not have such a program. Among the notable findings of Putbrese's survey were the following:

- Advisory programs may have a more positive impact on girls than boys.

- Advisory programs give students a feeling of more control over decisions.

- Advisory programs promote an atmosphere of equality.

- Advisory programs improve the sharing of feelings among students.

- Advisory programs may reduce the incidence of smoking and alcohol use.

In 1986 Connors conducted a detailed study of an ongoing advisory program in Sarasota, Florida, called Prime Time. The study determined that the program:

1. Helped students in their social growth.

2. Contributed to a positive school environment.

3. Helped students learn about the school.

4. Helped students learn to make friends.

5. Helped students learn how to get along with others.

6. Enhanced the teacher-student relationship.

7. Provided the advisors the opportunity to know students on a one-to-one basis.

8. Helped students develop a sense of positive self-worth.

9. Helped students acquire and improve the habits and attitudes necessary for responsible citizenship.

The study also found that when advisory was implemented along with the other basic middle school components, the average daily attendance increased as did standardized test scores. Also noted was this finding:

> Overall, the administrative staff and faculty have also seen a remarkable decrease in discipline problems, office referrals, and truancy. One teacher stated, 'In the past, on the last day of school, students would leave yelling obscenities from the busses but now students are sad that school has ended and leave with tears in their eyes and positive remarks.' Evidence that the program makes a difference. (p. 46)

Two comments made recently by students in Los Angeles in response to the question, "Does advisory help you feel connected to school?" are typical and in a similar vein. A seventh grade girl remarked: "Without advisory school would be more distant. It would not be as cheerful. We would not be as connected to everybody." And an eighth grade boy said,

Everyone in the school shares that bond that everyone has an advisor. So, from the 6th grade to 12th grade, everyone shares that connection with one teacher, and I think that everyone throughout the day has opened up to someone. It gets you into the state of mind that school is not only about work, but that it is a place where teachers really know you and understand you. So, I think, as a school, having advisory connects everybody.

(Shulkind & Foote, 2009)

Joel Murillo, Director of Middle School at Wildwood School, a highly regarded private school in Los Angeles, credits the school's advisory program with helping kids find their way. Students start every day in advisory, reviewing coursework, learning time management and organizational skills, and forming friendships. "Advisory is a sanctuary," Joel says. "Kids build relationships and trust, find the support they need, and learn to give support as well" (Wildwood, 2011).

Throughout the remaining chapters other answers to the question, "Why advisory?" will appear, but there is no doubt about the value and importance of advisory done well. It is so in keeping with the nature and needs of young adolescents.

Survey of North American middle schools

The Advisory Survey of North American Middle Grades Schools that we carried out in the spring of 2008 was in response to a recognition that little research had been done recently on what, why, and how advisory was being conducted (Burns, Behre-Jenkins, Kane, Tenorio, &Maestas, 2009). We knew from NMSA surveys of American middle schools conducted by Alexander, McEwin, and colleagues that some advisory structure was reported in-place in up to 60 percent of responding schools but had limited accompanying information (Alexander, McEwin, 1989; McEwin, Dickinson, & Jenkins, 1995, 2003).

The development and scope of our 2008 survey is shown in the following figures.

Figure 2.3

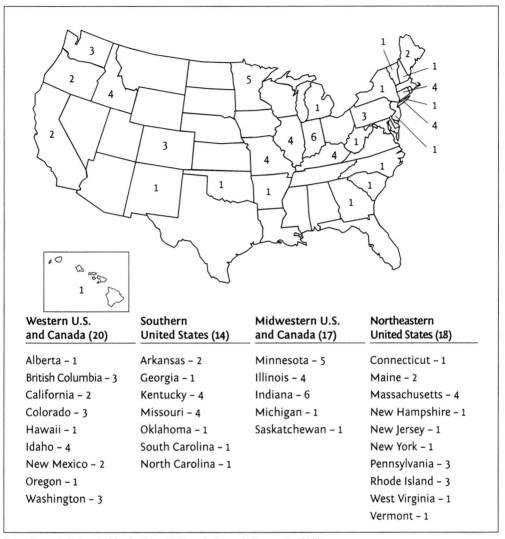

Western U.S. and Canada (20)	Southern United States (14)	Midwestern U.S. and Canada (17)	Northeastern United States (18)
Alberta – 1	Arkansas – 2	Minnesota – 5	Connecticut – 1
British Columbia – 3	Georgia – 1	Illinois – 4	Maine – 2
California – 2	Kentucky – 4	Indiana – 6	Massachusetts – 4
Colorado – 3	Missouri – 4	Michigan – 1	New Hampshire – 1
Hawaii – 1	Oklahoma – 1	Saskatchewan – 1	New Jersey – 1
Idaho – 4	South Carolina – 1		New York – 1
New Mexico – 2	North Carolina – 1		Pennsylvania – 3
Oregon – 1			Rhode Island – 3
Washington – 3			West Virginia – 1
			Vermont – 1

From, Burns J., Behre-Jenkins J., Kane, T., Tenorio, M, and Maestas, D. (2009).

Our 2008 questionnaire began with demographic questions to describe the size, shape, and character of the respondent schools. Figure 2.3 reveals the geographic distribution of the 69 respondent schools from a combined total of 28 U.S. states and Canadian provinces. The respondent sites were dominantly suburban (49%), with a 6-8 grade configuration in the vast majority (76%). The average student population was 678 with a total survey population totaling 46,111 students. Of the 69 respondent sites, 68 reported having a functioning advisory system. As we explore different approaches and aspects of advisory in subsequent chapters, we will present relevant data from this study.

3

What Do We Do in Advisory?
The Curriculum Question

Advisory is not a curriculum to be covered but a relationship to be nurtured.

What actually happens in advisory? What should happen? Could happen? Consider the following vignettes.

> George DiBuono, an award-winning art teacher at Holdrum Middle School, spent a lot of time helping his male advisory group develop social skills such as how to knot a necktie, how to set a table, and how to act in a restaurant.

> Advisors at Memorial Middle School used the showcase in the lobby to display personal hobbies and interests. Included were photography and artwork of several teachers, miniature figures made from wood, and the fire gear of a volunteer firefighter. The displays generated conversations between students and teachers about avocations and hobbies. During advisory, teachers, and sometimes students, shared their hobbies.

> When Nancy Doda visited a classroom, she noticed a number of cardboard boxes filled with odd pieces of cloth. Curious, she asked the teacher what all the material was for. The teacher responded that the boxes contained her advisory program. Each year her advisory group creates a quilt, she explained, and quilt making leads to "dialogue while doing." While their hands are busy quilting, advisor and advisees informally discuss numerous topics, whatever is on their minds or is a current concern. Her students essentially create their own curriculum.

The popular program "Don't Laugh at Me," designed by Peter, Paul, and Mary for middle level students, was the basis for the fall advisory in the sixth grades of one school district.

_____

In an Oregon middle school, the mid-morning advisory group conducted mock student-led conferences in preparation for their upcoming real student-led conferences, which were organized and implemented through the advisory program.

_____

An Albuquerque middle school principal celebrates Principal's Advisory Day when her students meet a school improvement goal established earlier in the week. If she announces on Thursday afternoon that the week's goal has been met, the next morning's advisory is an open house—popcorn machine popping away in the lobby with students free to socialize and visit each other's advisory classes—along with reminders to keep the building neat and show their best social behavior.

These examples illustrate the breadth of activities that can be considered "curriculum" for an advisory program. Curriculum in advisory certainly is different from the academic curriculum. Advisory almost never has a discrete body of material that must be covered and seldom involves direct instruction. Basically, advisory is all about the constructive use of time to produce

- Sound, positive relationships between students and adults.

- Positive relationships among groups of students and positive relationships among student groups and faculty and staff.

- Positive growth in students' social, emotional, and personal development.

In an ideal world, classes would be small, and adults and young adolescents could readily come to know one another well. In such a world of small classes and relatively homogenous populations, developing positive relationships would be no big deal. However, in our world of good-sized classes and diverse students with many needs ranging to the extreme, an advisory program is all but essential to the development of the healthy relationships that support learning and growth and a school-wide sense of community.

Early efforts to establish an advisory curriculum

As schools first worked to develop a sound, manageable, and developmentally appropriate curriculum for advisory, no model existed, so experimentation took place. There was a hurried effort to arrive at a curriculum because this new idea of advisory scared teachers. Forcefully, teachers pointed out that they weren't counselors, and they simply couldn't take on another preparation! Teachers whose authority was tied up in their subject matter expertise felt uncomfortable when, as they saw it, they would have to "rap" with kids about their problems and feelings related to growing up.

In response to these very common concerns, activities were quickly collected and assembled as handouts and distributed to teachers. Although these lessons may have provided advisors needed comfort and security, the mostly paper and pencil activities all too quickly became the routine. The over-use of canned worksheet activities, such as the ubiquitous Coat of Arms, shut out the informal, personal conversations that, theoretically, are at the heart of advisory. Such activities are by no means bad. Often, they are just what is needed to get a good discussion going or to present a dilemma that will push students to think deeply. They have a rightful place in any advisory program, but they should not comprise the entire curriculum.

Too often, advisors replaced these canned activities with more academic or quasi-academic events such as scripted study skills sessions, even study hall. This led to a quick downward spiral. If we had a quarter for each teacher who told us a story about turning away from advisory aims—"My students and I just couldn't get into those packaged advisory activities, so now we just use advisory time for study hall"—we would have lots of jukebox change.

Engaging young adolescents in conversations about their friendships, their social and emotional changes, and their positive and negative school experiences may seem less important than activities that resemble the more familiar academic curriculum, but this is not so. Advisory lays the groundwork and builds the foundation of relational support and self-understanding needed for students to succeed academically. Using an academic-type curriculum in advisory diverts time from the important directly relational activities.

Emerging as basics in an advisory curriculum were topics that related directly to the affective domain along with some that could be classified as academically oriented. Common topics included: self-esteem, friendships, non-verbal communication, group dynamics, peer pressure, S.S.R. (sustained, silent reading) or D.E.A.R. (drop everything and read), problem solving, goal setting, and career exploration. The range of what constitutes curriculum, as set forth in the opening vignettes, is virtually unlimited. However, because advisory was specifically added to fill an acknowledged gap in the almost exclusively cognitive oriented curriculum, affective topics or concerns were the highest priority.

The term "pastoral care" was often used with these early advisory programs that focused on affective concerns. An advisor was seen as a shepherd, watching over the growth and development of a "flock" of students. This term, however, was shied away from because, apparently, it had a religious connotation. In England, Australia, and New Zealand, however, the term has long been used and, in fact, it is almost considered a synonym for advisory itself.

The following materials on Australia's pastoral care program provide an excellent example of the type of curriculum that developed early in the United States and is still commonly found. These topics are almost foundational areas in advisory programs.

Pastoral care programs in Australia

There are actually very few free-standing middle schools in Australia; more typically, primary schools serve reception (kindergarten) through year seven, while secondary schools have grades eight through twelve (Aussie students are about a year younger than their American counterparts in the same numbered year). But whether in separate middle schools or not, Australian educators and policy makers tuned into young adolescents' needs for more than just academics and used a developmental focus on young adolescents that led to shepherding students with pastoral care programs. Australian educators provide effective pastoral care for their middle years students. They refused to accept an either/or mentality of academics-versus-developmental needs—they chose *both*!

Note: The material on the Australian advisory programs was prepared by Paul Deering, University of Hawaii, and Michael Hudson, Mary Asikas, David Lang, and Carl Lang, Australian educators.

Australian advisory programs are, like the country's vast landscape, varied, but all programs include an intentional focus on students' affective needs. For instance, the Seaford 6-12 School's advisory program (2009) has the following areas as emphases:

- School transition, acclimation

- Social and emotional resiliency

- Building positive relationships

- Prevention of substance abuse

- Healthy sexual/gender identity

- Bullying prevention and intervention

- Dropout prevention

- General student support/good shepherding

- Academic support and decision making.

Full-service pastoral care

The key to effective pastoral care is *relationships* built on caring and respect, which is in line with the thesis advanced by the authors of this book, that advisory is essentially relational. Australian schools, both primary and secondary, take pastoral care seriously and devote substantial time to planning, faculty development, and program implementation. A prime example is the previously mentioned Seaford 6-12 School, which opened in 1996. Seaford was designed and built to deliver on the recommendations of the *Junior Secondary Review* (Eyers, Cormack & Barratt, 1992)—which could be termed South Australia's *Turning Points* report. Pastoral care was an immediate and ongoing priority at Seaford and evolved into a broad-based program termed *Pathways and Futures* (P & F).

Scheduled every Wednesday for ninety minutes, P & F is structured in five-week blocks over a two-year cycle. Seaford teachers draw extensively upon *MindMatters* (2009) strategies, *Quality Learning Tools* (Langford International, 2009), and their years of teaching experience. P & F starts with a "getting to know you" unit to build relationships and establish a code of cooperation. The topics and five-week units in the middle school's P & F include those listed below. Students' accomplishments in the P & F units are shared with parents and community members in student-led conferences (SLCs). SLCs have become quite common in Australia as in the United States, and Seaford's educators find them to be crucial for student self-assessment, connecting with parents, and as a forum for discussion of all stakeholders' concerns and needs.

Figure 3.1

Pathways and Futures Five-Week Units

Independent Learning Plan (ILP) – The first unit introduces P & F and covers development of individualized digital plans for student curriculum, career paths, and support systems.

Conflict Resolution – Students learn through direct instruction and role playing; topics include strategies for negotiating a win-win, avoiding violence and abuse, and resolving conflict.

Bullying and Cyber-Bullying – Instruction is geared to changing the culture to non-acceptance of bullying; students explore websites to identify cyber-bullying and work through the issues as a class.

Sexual Health and Relationships Education (SHARE) – Developed by a government-contracted health organization, this school-wide program focuses on all aspects of healthy human relationships.

Mandated Child Protection – Local police are involved in a unit on child safety networking. Topics include the Youth Justice System, Graffiti in the City, and Legal Issues Out in the Community.

Drugs and Alcohol – A unit addressing tobacco, alcohol, marijuana, and hard drugs combines information, risk avoidance strategies, and student-raised issues.

Mental Health – This unit addresses what it means to be a healthy young person, plus issues such as autism, depression, anorexia, and more.

As students progress from Seaford's middle school to the secondary level in Year 9, the program goes deeper in several areas: drug and alcohol risk avoidance and treatment; and course and career counseling, including identification of three or more careers of interest. At the senior level of Years 10-12, students develop a *Personalized Learning Plan*, which enables them to identify several career paths, including the subjects and skills required to attain those careers. The plan also helps them establish school completion goals, including identification of literacy and numeracy strengths and weaknesses and strategies for addressing them.

Involvement of the school's counselors in all aspects of Seaford's pastoral care program was essential to its success. Since 2004, the school has annually administered the Social Outcomes Survey (Queensland Government, 2002) to all students. Percentages of students reporting highly positive outlooks have been in the mid-70s to upper-80s on all seven criteria since 2005, with the first year's data being about 10 points lower. The seven criteria are: self confidence; relating to others; interest in learning; commitment to community; work readiness; understanding social order; and optimism for the future. Academic outcomes are similarly strong, with from 75 to 90 percent of Year 7 and Year 9 students achieving proficiency on standardized tests of literacy and numeracy (Seaford 6-12 School, 2008). Such excellence has brought considerable renown, as Seaford and/or its professionals won two awards each year in 2007, 2008, and 2009.

Targeting bullying

The issue of bullying in Australian schools was analyzed recently in the Australian *Covert Bullying Prevalence Study* (Cross, Shaw, Hearn, Epstein, Monks, Lester, & Thomas, 2009), which surveyed over 20,000 students and nearly 500 staff in over 200 schools. The study examined both the hidden, covert forms of bullying, as well as more open, overt forms. Covert bullying was defined as:

> any form of aggressive behaviour that is repeated, intended to cause harm and characterised by an imbalance of power, and is 'hidden', out of sight of, or unacknowledged by adults. Covert bullying includes behaviours linked to social aggression, relational aggression and indirect aggression.... (p. xxi)

Among the key findings were that 70 percent of school staff members reported having observed overt or covert bullying. With young adolescents, rates of victimization hovered around 30 percent, while under ten percent reported being perpetrators. Cyber-bullying was also examined, with just under 10 percent of students and staff reporting awareness of such incidents. As with other adolescent developmental changes, girls were found to begin cyber-bullying a couple years ahead of boys and were more prone to engage in covert versus overt forms of bullying.

In Queensland and elsewhere, legislation exists to protect and prevent students from harm in schools. David Lang and Carl Lang have had very positive experiences with *Acting Against Bullying* (O'Toole & Burton, 2009), a program that uses drama to allow students to act out, analyze, and resolve bullying scenarios. In groups of three, students create or are given a context in which they act out the roles of bullies, victims, and bystanders. They begin with a freeze-frame representing a bullying situation, and develop this into a role play, trying different strategies for resolving the problem. At designated stages, peer audience members may speak to the characters in role, suggest strategies, swap places with participants, or inquire about participants' thoughts, feelings and approaches.

Students learn in *Action Against Bullying* (AAB) to identify and work through the three stages of bullying—latent, emerging, and manifest. This helps them realize that bullying rarely occurs in a random or isolated context, but is usually the product of earlier, escalating events. Recognizing these initial events and signs allows students to address a potential bullying incident before it manifests itself. It is here that the power of the bystander(s) comes to the fore, as students can help friends who are at risk of bullying with helpful strategies and provide a network of support.

The keys to AAB's effectiveness are twofold. For one, students direct and lead the process, and hence, are empowered to assess situations and take action. Secondly, AAB eschews blaming which leads to gridlock; instead, it encourages students to take action. David and Carl advocate starting the program with older students, e.g., Year 11 and 12s, and then have them model and mentor the processes with middle grades peers. In this way, a senior school can "grow its own" school-wide resources for preventing and addressing bullying, and building resilience.

The implementation of AAB by the Langs, their colleagues, and students are quite consistent with the recommendations of the National Middle School Association, which stated in its research summary on bullying:

> School-wide intervention programs led by caring adults with high expectations and an actively engaging curriculum that includes meaningful literature, collaborative learning, and service learning activities are specific strategies that appear to foster resiliency in victims of bullying. (Lorimer, 2006, p. 2)

AAB is very popular with students who have found the strategies to be useful and effective in resolving bullying situations. Evaluation research by Bruce Burton (2008), one of AAB's developers, offers further evidence of its effectiveness, with student surveys indicating that from two-thirds to nearly 100 percent of program participants report that they can identify the stages of bullying, are more likely to intervene in bullying situations, and believe that bullying can be defused.

Anyone interested in additional information about these programs can contact Paul Deering (deering@hawaii.edu), Mary Asikas (Mary.Asikas @seafordhs.sa.edu.au), or Carl Lang (carl_uhuru@yahoo.com.au).

The use of themes to structure curriculum.

As advisory programs began to take hold back in the U.S., structured curriculum was needed to enable all the advisors in a school to carry out essentially the same program and to communicate its nature to parents and others. Over the years, themes evolved as one way to structure a program. Themes allowed schools to take advantage of rather wide-open content possibilities, but still structure programs sufficiently, so they could be readily understood and followed by the advisors. Establishing monthly themes based on the nature of the school calendar is one approach. For example, in all schools establishing friendships and other relationships will be addressed one way or another during the first month of school. This cultural phenomenon of emerging adolescence is a group process. For the very reason that it is so natural, many schools leave it to chance, which can result in formation of new, positive friendships but leaves students unsupported in dealing with cliques, bullies, or gangs. Mid-August through mid-September is, for students, very much about identity (individual and group) and provides a natural advisory theme to start the year.

The table below ties the school months to some natural, cultural milestones that can serve as themes. We've linked a guiding question with each theme. As previously stated, we don't think advisory benefits from a prescribed curriculum of daily lesson plans, but the school's academic curriculum is rich with possibilities for advisory themes that will provide needed structure and be supportive of ongoing academic studies.

Table 3.1

Guiding Questions for Themes

Months	Theme	Guiding Question
Aug.–Sept.	Identity	Who am I? What are my interests?
Sept.–Oct.	Success	What am I good at?
Oct.–Nov.	Service	How can I make a difference locally?
Nov.–Dec.	Celebration	How do we celebrate life?
Jan.–Feb.	Careers	What do I want to become?
Feb.–Mar.	Goals	What are my academic goals?
Mar.–Apr.	Service	How can I make a difference globally?
Apr.–May	Friendship	How do I demonstrate friendship?
May–June	Completion	How do we recognize growth and closure?

Themes throughout the year can coincide with seasonal emphases such as food drives in November, a career focus in mid-winter, gearing up for standardized testing in February, and closure rituals in May. Consider a global focus in April, possibly supporting life-saving clean water projects in underdeveloped areas or another project tied to geography or science.

Another general type of theme sometimes used to structure programs is citizenship or character education. A specific character trait such as responsibility, honesty, or integrity becomes the focus for a week. There are commercially prepared materials available that support such efforts. Educators for Social Responsibility (www.esrnational.org) provides many resources for advisory programs that are concerned with building safe, caring, and equitable classrooms and schools. Peter Yarrow, of Peter, Paul, and Mary fame, has created the program "Don't Laugh at Me" for grades 6–8 that is available at no cost (http://www.operationrespect.org/pdf/guide.pdf). Dealing with self-respect, conflict resolution, and ways to counter bullying, this excellent online program fits perfectly in advisory. Another very effective resource that engages students and leads to meaningful discussions of personal and moral traits is the more recently released Film Clips for Character Education series. Using short excerpts from popular Hollywood films like *Shrek* or *Remember the Titans*, the program engages students in considering character traits such as sportsmanship, empathy, and perseverance (www.FilmclipsOnline.com).

The Atlanta City Schools have implemented a system-wide advisory program that focuses on four areas: career exploration, career awareness, academic support, and like skills. The film clips fit especially well in their life skills component and teachers are pleased with their effectiveness. Teachers also report that they are great stand-alones, or they can be used as parts of a larger unit.

Community service projects

While service-learning has always been associated with middle schools, its emphasis has increased substantially over the last two decades. National organizations committed to service-learning have formed, presidents have been advocates for its expansion in schools, and the professional literature has reflected this newfound belief in the educational value of community-based service projects. Such projects are most appropriate curriculum for an advisory program and often become a regular and ongoing component of programs.

Our survey revealed that many students and faculty engage in community service outside their schools. More than one-third of the respondents (38 percent) reported substantial engagement in stewardship activities not related to school. When conducted through a school's advisory program, however, service-learning projects can be more enduring and have greater educational value. For instance, the advisory groups of a grade might carry out a year-long project working with the local recreational association that would include physical work on the playing fields and facilities and related efforts to advance sportsmanship and participation. Such projects can tie into the ongoing work of interdisciplinary teams. In the above example, for instance, considerable mathematics would be involved in measuring the fields, angles, and distances. The teams might also study how community recreational programs are funded and maintained or carry out a related project researching the safety and health issues of contact sports for young adolescents. There are many opportunities for young adolescents to experience new and positive learnings through engaging in service-learning in their advisory programs. No program, it would seem, should be without such experiences.

Communicating with parents and guardians

One major goal of any advisory program has to be to serve as a communication link with parents, guardians, and families and bring about their always-desired but hard-to-achieve involvement. Doing so is important as parental involvement traditionally drops off significantly when students leave the elementary school, yet research studies have shown there is a direct correlation between the degree of parental involvement and student achievement. The advisory program is in a particularly favorable position, then, to counter the traditional drop-off in parental involvement and gain the academic benefit that comes with sustained parental involvement. With a limited number of families involved in an advisory group, so much more can be done than when a teacher has up to a hundred families to contact.

The advisor should, of course, be recognized as the prime contact for parents seeking information about any aspect of their youngster's education, In most cases, the advisor will be taking the initiative to contact parents, share information, and solicit any concerns parents might have. A home visit early on and a phone call or letter before the school year begins is always in order. When talking with parents, let the parents do most of the talking, sharing their perceptions of their child and their hopes for him or her.

Regular one-on-one conferences between advisees and their advisor is a necessary early step and a foundation for carrying out the desired parent-student-advisor conferences and related activities that will involve families. Advisors should hold four or more individual advisor-advisee conferences throughout the year and two student-parent-advisor conferences a year, usually on school days completely devoted to such conferences.

Many schools have established a parent and family room with materials and resources and comfortable seating for reviewing materials and holding conferences. If such a facility is not available, perhaps by combining efforts, the advisors can create one. Advisors can send books, articles, and materials on the academic program home regularly with the advisees, by U. S. mail, or by e-mail. As advisors get to know their advisees' parents and family, they will likely discover areas of expertise possessed by an adult that can be utilized in an advisory activity or in the instructional program. Capitalize of these possibilities whenever possible.

The effective monitoring of an advisee's academic progress calls for a definite plan. Such a plan has to developed in cooperation with the interdisciplinary teams. While the distribution of the report card and any interim reports should be done by the advisors, more is called for in a plan that advisors develop to fulfill the special responsibility and opportunity they have to involve families in the educational enterprise. A rather unusual activity related to family involvement occurred in Jeannette Stern's advisory. The advisory group of this veteran educator in Wantagh Middle School, New York, together held a baby shower for an advisee's expecting mother and new stepfather. Stern's advisory has also visited hospitals, made get-well cards, gone to wakes, and paid shivah calls—all things that students do not feel comfortable doing alone, but unfortunately, on occasions, need to do (Education World, 2004).

Activities combining advisory groups

An effective curriculum in an advisory program can and should include activities that involve two or more advisory groups working together. Some friendly competition between groups is always in order. Perhaps a volleyball game, a tug of war, a spelling bee, or a geography countdown. On the cooperation side, activities calling for the involvement of two or more advisory groups include service-learning, landscaping projects, visits to nursing homes, and other substantial projects that likely have an academic component. Often, all the advisory groups of a particular grade may work together on a project, or in small schools, all the advisory groups may participate in one activity.

Some activities call for more minds rather than just more hands. Two teachers, Gary Jones and Mae Benson, discovered this by accident. One day Gary let Mae's advisees join his group, so she that could attend an IEP conference. When the conference was ultimately cancelled and Mae came back a few minutes later, an animated discussion about the responsibilities of babysitting for hire was in progress. The very active exchanges, first initiated by Gary—who was soon observing from the sidelines—focused on what it was okay and not okay to take from the client family's refrigerator.

As the 25-minute advisory ended too soon, the advisees went on to their third-period elective. Gary and Mae looked at one another as Mae asked, "Why can't I get discussions going like that one?" Gary laughed and said, "I honestly don't know. My group is never that responsive." As they looked at one another with that question in their minds, a realization set in—they had just stumbled upon something powerful. They came to call it "critical mass," meaning that for some discussions to be effective, a larger group is needed!

Experimenting informally, they met once a week with the paired group. By the end of that year, they had extended the paired activity from topical discussions to planning stewardship projects together and breaking out into subdivided groups, with Mae and Gary leading different activities. Two notable outcomes of that first year of pairing were (1) the word got out and students in the seventh grade wanted to join Gary or Mae's advisory, and (2) their 25-minute advisory began to seem too short. Noting their success, the principal asked them to do a presentation about paired advisory during the school's August professional development days.

At mid-morning advisory time on Tuesdays and Thursdays, these two groups combine in Mae's language arts classroom or Gary's life science room. Their combined seventh grade advisees form a group of 30. In Gary's room, some congregate in circles on the floor, while others sit on corners of the solid tables. Socializing as they wait for the day's activities to begin, they eat granola bars or sliced fruit. On occasion, they stay in the large group for a 25-minute "town meeting" to discuss team rules, review policies, and make plans. Planning is a big part of advisory. During each quarter, they plan for major team- or school-based events—pep rallies, community stewardship projects, dances, and career fairs.

Mae states, "When I first started advisory, the idea of building relationships with young people was daunting. But when we discovered the role of student voice in important events—things important to them—the quality of relationships really grew. Now, a lot of the time, I stand by and watch." She adds, "Sometimes my role is active, and, at times, I do have to rein in our 'Queen Bees' or 'Alpha Males.' After all, these are regulation 12- and 13-year-olds. Yet, by having students in charge of planning, they not only develop responsibility and skills with democratic action, the whole relationship thing takes care of itself."

The concept of partner teaming is not new, although its primary use has been to help new advisors by pairing them with veterans for a period of time. But in a few schools, partner-led advisories, usually of twenty or more students, have been the modus operandi for many years, and this practice merits further consideration. It is also a good idea for every advisory group to have a designated partner group that can be included in a particular project or activity at a moment's notice.

Advisory five-days-a-week

Perhaps the most successful programs develop when a five-days-a-week period is regularly scheduled. Having a period of thirty-or-so minutes available each day offers opportunities for significant advisory-related experiences. Affectively-oriented activities can be scheduled one or two days, mini-courses on another day, and perhaps intramurals, clubs, student government, career-related sessions, or an assembly on other days. The possibilities for providing enrichment experiences and activities that cater to student interests are great when such a period is scheduled. Every middle school should have such a period. When one reviews the goals of the middle school, it is hard to see how they can all be met without such a period.

An excellent example is provided by DePere Middle School in Wisconsin. The established advisory period, called FleXtime, offered opportunites for enrichment, academic support, and typical advisory activities. The schedule for the month of March at DePere shows how this period was used. Note the summary at the end that identifies how FleXtime was used for academic, social-emotional, and housekeeping purposes.

Month of March Grade 7 FleXtime

Mar. 2 –	Read Across America Day. Read one or two of Dr.Suess's books aloud on his birthday.
Mar. 5 –	Self-esteem video; all house students in the auditeria.
Mar. 6 –	Finish the hands activity in the auditeria; wrap-up video.
Mar. 7–	Read aloud Paulsen's novel Harris and Me (2007).
Mar. 8 –	Locker clean out.
Mar. 9 –	End of the quarter work day.
Mar. 12–16 –	Random Acts of Kindness interest activities.
Mar. 19 –	Alhohol, Tobacco, and Drug Abuse (ATODA) presentation; all house students in auditeria.

Mar. 20 –	ATODA presentation follow-up.
Mar. 21 –	Custodial Day project.
Mar. 22–23 –	It's spring! Organize and deliver Random Acts of Kindness gifts.
Mar. 26 –	Peer conference writing piece with eighth grade writing class.
Mar. 27 –	Peer/self-revision with eighth grade class.
Mar. 28 –	Continue reading aloud the novel Harris and Me.
Mar. 29–30 –	Display case to show our Random Acts of Kindness gifts.

Summary of Time Use in March FleXtime

Academic	8 days
Social-Emotional	12 days
Housekeeping	1 day

(Rottier, et al., 2009, p. 26)

Final thoughts on curriculum

In many respects, the word "curriculum," as generally perceived, doesn't fit what takes place in an advisory program. Curriculum usually refers to content, the course of study, what students are to master, and on what they will be evaluated. As you reflect on the array of ideas, materials, and activities—all optional and just possibilities—presented in this chapter, "curriculum" just doesn't seem to be the right term. But if you go back to the original meaning of the word curriculum, you will discover that it may, indeed, fit. Originally, the word didn't have anything to do with school at all but rather was the Latin word for "race-course." Bobbitt, in 1918, first used this term that identified a physical layout, such as one for chariot racing, to apply to a school's program. Interesting, but certainly, as presented in this chapter, the word curriculum applied to advisory might well be replaced with a different label.

In advisory, we refer more to things that are to be experienced rather than learned, activities designed more to shape attitudes than achievement. Advisory's lessons are acquired slowly over time rather than being the result of one or more daily lesson plans. Decisions about what to do in advisory can't be made on the basis of an approved course of study or state standards. This is the beauty of advisory, but it calls for decisions that require professional educators to have in mind the realities and a full understanding of their students, their colleagues, and their community as well as their own philosophy of education. Deciding on curriculum for advisory is a tough assignment. There are no cookbook recipes to follow, but being able to plan what is to be done in advisory allows us to serve young adolescents in ways we know will make a difference. Actually that last sentence needs to be revised because, ultimately, the best curriculum for advisees is the one planned by the advisees themselves! While initially the advisor will plan and initiate various activities to pursue, as the group coalesces and becomes a small learning community of trusted and trusting individuals, the group will increasingly decide how best to use its time together. And so it should be. However, the advisor never relinquishes his or her professional and legal responsibility and simply turns the group loose on its own. The advisor's voice and its influence are still a part of discussions, although not the known-to-begin-with determining voice that teachers usually possess.

4

Organizational Considerations: How Many, How Often, How Long, Who

If advisory doesn't show up as time in the schedule, it's not valued.
Is English valued? Yes. How do I know? It's in the schedule.
Is math valued? Yes. How do I know? It's in the schedule.
Is advisory valued? Well, let's take a look at the schedule and see.
If it's in the schedule, it's valued. If it isn't in the schedule, it's not valued!

—Ross Burkhardt

Whether you choose a structure such as a looped advisory or the more common independent, grade-based organization or some variation for your advisory, you will need to make a number of critical organizational decisions, including where to place advisory in the schedule, as the statement from Ross Burkhardt emphasizes. This chapter will examine organizational matters applicable to any program plan your school decides to implement. The size of the groups, length of period, number of meetings, grouping of students, selection of advisors, and leadership of the advisory program are all inter-related, and they all relate to the content discussed in the previous chapter. Keeping all of this and the program goals in mind is a task for a master juggler—it requires keeping six or seven balls in the air at the same time.

What size advisory groups?

Although we have indicated there are no hard-and-fast rules when considering middle grades advisory, we offer one here that comes close—smaller is better! Experts all agree that smaller advisory groups, between 10 and 15 students per advisor, are best (Burkhardt & Kane, 2005; Burns, 2007; Connors, 1992; Galassi, Gulledge, & Cox, 1998; Hoverstein, Doda, & Lounsbury, 1991; James &

Spradling, 2002; Spear, 2005; Stevenson, 2002). In fact, we could not locate any source that even suggested the advisability of creating larger advisory groups. The benefits of small groups, roughly half the size of most regular classes, are obvious to any experienced teacher.

Achieving the desired small groups, however, inevitably presents some problems. Dividing a student body into groups of 12, with all certified personnel serving as advisors, would result in a 1 to 12 ratio in the case of most schools. But actually using all certified persons may not be possible or even advisable, so compromises will likely be necessary. Consider the result of dividing a team of four teachers and 110 students into equal-size groups: the resulting advisories of 27 or 28 are too large, so, perhaps, several exploratory teachers could be brought in to serve as advisors. On the other hand, if the teams were multiage teams that would remain together over three years, the larger number might be acceptable. A group larger than 15 might also be defensible if the groups met four or five days a week for a period of 25 to 30 minutes. Keep in mind the small-is-better principle as you work your way through the scheduling details, but recognize that Utopian-size groups are not always possible.

How often should advisories meet?

Closely related to the size of the group is the issue of how often they should meet. Before responding to that question, however, let's look at an excellent, large-scale, long-term holistic research study that provides support for having an advisory program that meets regularly for a half hour or so. This landmark study compared "emergent or merely proficient" middle schools with "higher performing" middle schools. Robert Felner and his associates (1997) found that middle schools with advisory meetings of 30 to 45 minutes four or five times a week had substantially higher levels of student achievement and significantly reduced school-related stress for both teachers and students than schools with a less evident advisory commitment, as indicated by less frequent and shorter meetings. Keep this research finding in mind; it has been supported by other studies and has become an accepted principle. Too often, positive and immediate results are expected from a very limited advisory program, but where a sound program has been in operation for some time, positive results will become evident.

Our own 2008 status survey revealed that, among those middle grades schools with active advisory programs, a clear majority (54%) reported having advisory meetings four or five times per week (Burns et al., 2009). Among all the other frequencies of advisory meetings (which totaled 46%), the 19% of schools with once-a-week advisory were in the next-highest category. A random sample of all middle schools likely would show a much lower percentage of schools with programs that met four or five times per week.

The unfortunate reality is that hundreds of programs meet just once a week, and some, even fewer times. While limited commitment is a factor in advisories meeting infrequently, actually creating a period in the schedule for advisory is as much a problem. To avoid upsetting the entire schedule, minutes are often stolen from each academic period, the lunch period, and passing time—a doable but seldom well-received strategy. Since extending the school day to provide a period for advisory involves bus schedules and would require board action, it, too, is seldom pursued as an option, so creative administrators have found other ways to support an advisory program. A fairly common and seemingly sensible practice has been to extend the existing homeroom period once or twice a week to create a 25- to 30-minute period for advisory activities, shortening all class periods a few minutes each to make this possible. However, this practice, reflecting a timidity that doesn't bode well for the program, has generally proven unsatisfactory. Many schools, however, have been able to establish the desirable five-days-a-week period for advisory and related activities that opens up all sorts of exciting possibilities, as pointed out in Chapter 3.

How often advisories should meet is directly related to the question of how long the meetings should be and involves some combination of what is possible schedule-wise and what kind of activities are appropriate to meet the program's goals. Problem-solving activities may require more than 25 minutes to be effective, as would various challenges between advisory groups. Flexibility is always desirable. It all depends…

More than once-a-day meetings. While scheduling an advisory period every day is considered the standard from which one deviates as necessary, advisory may meet more than once a day! The merits of such a practice are many and should be recognized. Consider the benefits of starting every day with your advisees in a

20- to 30-minute period and then ending the day with them in a brief 5- to 7-minute period. Middle level teachers, conscious of the problems young adolescents have with organizing, can immediately see the benefits of this bit of shepherding. Burns uses the example of Vega de Sol (a composite of several actual schools) shows how extended advisory times create various benefits to the advisor/advisee relationship:

> At Vega del Sol, a grades 6–8 charter school in a semi-rural county of New Mexico, students meet with their advisors a minimum of twice each day. The school's conceptual model is built on self-reliance and relational bonds across age levels. The school's students belong to one of two multiage core teams, each of which is led by a pair of partner-teachers. In addition to the academic core, all students take music or art and physical education. Each day begins at 7:50 a.m., when advisors and advisees meet for 20 minutes to greet, to socialize, and especially to organize for the day. Each of the full-time faculty, including the director (principal-teacher), led one 12–13 member cross-age advisory group. (Burns, 2007)

Starting each day with advisory is hardly unique, but what happens at mid-day at VdS, makes it stand apart in terms of scheduled commitment to advisory.

> At 11:45 a.m. students and advisors meet at their designated advisory space for the 20 minutes called advisory/lunch. (Faculty have 30 minutes of duty-free lunch either before or after the advisory/lunch, and all students also have semi-structured free time following their advisory/lunch).

It began as a short-term experiment:

> During VdS's third year, construction of the school's commons created many disruptions. Faculty agreed, albeit with some reluctance, to solve some space-related problems due to construction by having lunch with their advisees. Eight years later, the faculty speak as one in describing the tradition of advisory/lunch as not only a great idea, but as the place and time when high-quality interaction between students and their teachers occurs.

One faculty member informally evaluated the program in these statements:

> We come to know our advisees well enough that when we see them in other, seemingly "less consequential" times throughout the day— in classes, on the grounds, or in the hallway—we recognize them more as "members of

our (advisory) family," and we greet and acknowledge them as such. It has become its own tradition—comradeship based on advisory. It is unlike anything any one of us has experienced in other schools.

How long should advisory periods be?

The length of the advisory period, as mentioned previously, is likely to be determined more by how much time can be squeezed out of the strongly entrenched time commitments to the academic areas than by simply deciding what length of period would be most desirable. Quite often, this matter of finding adequate time for advisory is the largest single problem faced when instituting a program. Our survey revealed what might be encouraging information on the length of advisory periods in the North American schools that reported.

Figure 4.1

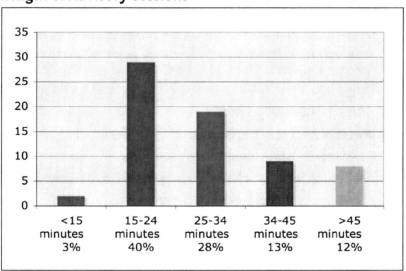

The vast majority of sites (68%) indicated committing between 15 and 34 minutes per advisory meeting, and an additional 25% committed to even longer periods. The largest single group (40%) of respondent sites had advisory meetings of 15 to 24 minutes. The length of the period tends to determine the kind of activities that can be carried out in a session.

One research finding from the 2008 status survey warrants highlighting. In the study, the 12% of respondents committing the greatest time per session (more than 45 minutes) were also among the schools reporting holding advisory once a week. This finding paired with data from Alexander and McEwin's 1988 national survey, along with 1993, 2001, and 2009 follow-up surveys conducted by McEwin and associates (McEwin, Dickinson, & Jenkins, 1995, 2003; McEwin & Greene, 2010), demonstrate a trend toward one-day-a-week advisories. Over 30 years, the number of schools reporting once-a-week advisories has doubled. While we advocate for frequent meetings of advisory, possibilities for meaningful once-a-week advisory activities should be explored.

Figure 4.2

Advisory Scheduling Trends 1988-Present

Survey Year	1988	1993	2001	2008*	2009
Once-per-week advisory	10%	14%	16%	19%*	18%

*Based on a small, non-representative response from 70 North American middle grades schools

Alexander & McEwin, 1988; McEwin, Dickinson, & Jenkins, 1995, 2003; Burns, Behre-Jenkins, Kane, Tenorio, & Maestas, 2009; McEwin & Greene, 2010.

When should advisory meet?

Usually this is not a big problem. Because advisory was inevitably thought of in relation to homeroom, which always starts the day, that is when most programs were originally scheduled. Scheduling advisory in the middle of the day may be preferable, but experience has proved that having advisory as the last period in the day is not appropriate. That time is not conducive to the kind of unhurried conversations and thinking together that are regularly a part of advisory. Psychologically, students, at that time of the day, aren't receptive to new materials or creative thinking. (Neither are teachers, which is the reason for rotating schedules.) Putting this short bit of time at the end of the day also fosters the notion that advisory isn't really that important. Perhaps most desirable is a rotating schedule of academic and advisory periods.

Where should advisory groups meet?

This question rarely gets any attention. Even in resources specifically dealing with advisory, this issue may not be discussed. And although it may not be as important a consideration as size or length of period, the location of the group's meetings can impact the effectiveness of the sessions. While any classroom can be used, the cohesiveness of the group and the climate for discussions can be enhanced if they have "a place of their own" where they always meet. There they can put up the flag, banner, or even the coat of arms they created. Its presence would say, in effect, "Meeting in session, do not disturb." This, of course, can be done even if they are located in a regular classroom.

There are rarely ample vacant spaces available in a middle school, but check out possibilities—one or two small preview or conference rooms in the media center; a corner of the lunch room; the ISS room; the computer lab; the band, chorus, and art rooms; even a dead-end hallway. There are bound to be some nooks and crannies in the school that would provide a home place for a group. Since the dozen or so advisees usually sit in a circle, the square footage needed is not great, and sitting on the floor is not only acceptable, it may be preferable.

How should students be divided into groups?

In the early years of the middle school movement, students were most often assigned randomly to teacher-based guidance. This practice was based on the belief that advisors should not be advisees' core teachers, those who had grading power over them. Randomness, it was felt, would keep the work of advisory tightly focused and separated from academic concerns. This "purified" view, however, didn't hold up very well, and, increasingly, other considerations impacted the process of establishing groups.

The survey data about assigning advisory groups are detailed in Figure 4.3.

Figure 4.3

How students are assigned to advisory groups

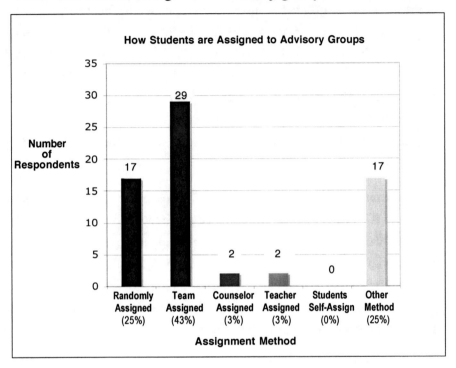

It is uncertain exactly how team-based assignments were carried out. It might have been alphabetically, at random, or by teacher choice or some combination of criteria. The 25% who selected "Other," as shown in the graph, gave qualitative responses, shown in Figure 4.4, which fall into general categories of "more purposeful placement" or "convenience."

Figure 4.4

Open-Ended Responses ("Other" responses in Figure 4.3)

Purposeful	Placed by administration and guidance
	Administratively assigned
	Counselor, teacher, parent input
	Random with some exceptions--kids who should not be together
	Random and counselor assignment (2x)
	Random and team-based (2x)
	Selected by teachers with help from previous year's teachers
	Team-based and recommendation of previous year's teachers
	All students attend a topical class
Convenience	By class
	First period teacher
	By homerooms
	Attached to core class

Note that most of the "other" responses point to even more purposeful design in placing students in advisory groupings.

When forming groups to align with your program's goals, using recommendations secured from the previous year's teachers would seem to make sense. Below is a list of student characteristics that last year's teachers could use in preparing their recommendations.

Figure 4.5

Advisee Descriptors

1. Which students have strong social skills and tend to thrive in any setting?

2. Which students tend to be school leaders?

3. Which students have some extraordinary ability or talent?

4. Which students absolutely need to be separated from which other students?

5. Which students would benefit from being grouped with a particular friend?

6. Which students tend to be loners?

8. Which students appear to have special needs?

9. Which students are on IEPs?

Then, each student's name is printed on a 5" x 7" note card. These cards are color coded by grade level. Entered on each card are the data provided by previous teachers. You might see that the card for Sally Otero, an eighth grader, is marked: 1, 3 "flute," 5 "Diane Keane". This tells that Sally will be an asset to most groups, she has a musical interest, and she would benefit from pairing with her friend Diane. When sorted from the other cards, students with this (or a similar configuration, such as 1, 2, and 3) might represent 60% to 80% of the students. Begin by sorting this block of students into advisory groups.

By attempting to place together certain good friends, we address a common complaint as cited by Chris Stevenson (2002):

> An eighth grader who felt alienated from her school because its organization method kept her separated from her friends said cynically, " I think they're just trying to keep us away from one another so we'll stay confused." (p. 107)

The next step is to carefully sort into emerging advisory groups the students who are identified as loners or isolates. Expect this to be a relatively small number, perhaps 5%; but these are students to be aware of and carefully assigned. Finally, we would place in different groups those students identified as "best not to be together" based on their behavior history.

Gender-based advisories. In the early years, single-gender advisories were often established based on the premise that many personal-social issues could best be considered in single-sex groups. This practice, though it had merit, did not last as a common practice. Recently, though, it has reappeared with the promotion of single-gender academic classes. More commonly, what has occurred, and should occur, is the creation of single-sex advisories for specific periods of time. Two advisory groups merge and then are divided into single-sex groups. This temporary grouping has often been used for sex education sessions but should be a frequent practice for other reasons. For instance, getting male and female points of view on various social issues and then having the larger co-ed group assemble to share their thoughts has merit. And simply extending the relationships of one group with another group helps to offset the criticism that advisory groups become too isolated and the "I never get to be with my friends" charge. After groups have had time to become a real little family, it is good practice to occasionally divide them back into two new groups (not on the basis of gender) to scramble them up for a session or two. Recall the experience of the two teachers related in Chapter 3 who discovered the importance of "critical mass" for some discussions.

Who should be, could be, advisors?

Theoretically, all professionally certified personnel are qualified to serve as advisors, but there are always considerations that limit that number. Some teachers may simply be unwilling or unable to assume this role, some can't participate due to schedules, and then there are some individuals who may be willing and able but are not certified personnel.

Realistically speaking, every middle grades teacher is really an advisor, whether consciously filling that role or not. Given the nature of young adolescents, anyone working with them is a model whose behavior is noted and thoughtfully considered and whose comments are often classifiable as advice. Teachers who are fulfilling the tenets of the middle school concept really cannot help but be advisors, and as middle level classrooms become more student-centered, the distinction between being a teacher and being an advisor will fade. Teachers in the exploratory program are, by nature, always well-suited to be advisors, as are coaches. In Chapter 6 more attention is given to the qualifications and preparation of teachers for this slightly different role of advisor.

There have been many cases of school secretaries serving as advisors, and some custodians have also successfully filled the role. A well-liked secretary or popular custodian often has the attributes needed to lead an advisory group. For non-certified individuals to be solely responsible for a student group, board of education approval would be needed, at the least. Most often, such individuals become co-advisors with a teacher.

Principals present a special case. Although they are usually willing and able, their time-intensive responsibilities make it difficult for them to be advisors. Again, they can be co-advisors and take on a somewhat larger group with a teacher or with another administrator. Serving as an advisor gives an administrator the regular personal contact with students that they desire but usually are unable to have.

Nesting advisory in teams

Often, advisory is included in the regular responsibilities of an interdisciplinary team, and all team members serve as advisors. When consciously integrated into teamed settings, advisory becomes less a structural element with its own separate time and place and emerges more in the daily interactions between teachers and learners on a team. When advisory is team-based,

- The number of interactions between advisors and advisees is maximized.

- The relationships between and among the team teachers improve.

- Any issues or concerns students (advisees) have are readily identified and can be dealt with in advisory.

One additional advantage has been pointed out by Rottier (2001):

> One of the major reasons for the difficulties advisory programs face is that many teachers do not feel comfortable addressing the kind of topics that inevitably arise in advisory programs. During team planning time, these concerns can be expressed and plans made accordingly. For example, one person on the team could specialize in a particularly sensitive or difficult topic like alcoholism, and, over a period of days, meet with all students on the team during the team activity period to provide leadership in exploring this important topic. (p. 146)

What we are describing is a holistic interaction—a melding of advisory with natural, daily opportunities to develop caring connections. As a result of this integration, the impact of advisory permeates all interactions throughout the day; team members' advisory actions, as a whole, exceed the sum of the parts—synergy happens.

We've heard teachers and administrators enthusiastically talk about the advantages of team-based advisory. For instance, a teacher in Vega del Sol Charter Middle School proclaimed:

> I loved it. It was the best because I got to see my advisees, kids I really liked, four or maybe five times each day. For example, I would see Jess first thing in advisory from 7:50 to 8:10 a.m. Then she was in my math class just before lunch. Because we partner-team at VdS, Jess was also in science class with me after lunch. Depending on the season and our expeditionary activities, I saw Jess more after the day's classes were through. (Burns, 2007)

De Pere Middle School in Wisconsin implemented a carefully designed merger of advisory and teaming in 2006, replacing an expanded homeroom program that was failing. The principal, Tammy Woulf, in the small book *Teaming and Advisory: Perfect Partners* (Rottier, Woulf, Bonettin, & Meyer, 2009), claims that the program "has been very effective in helping us reach the social, emotional, and academic needs of our students. The lessons are the product of team planning that produces creative and authentic learning opportunities for our students, ranging from team building, to drug prevention, to community service opportunities" (p. 44). Additionally, she says the program "has provided a vital opportunity for us to form relationships with our students, which is a fundamental component of the middle school philosophy." The book fully describes this model.

A major disadvantage of this full merger of advisory and teaming is that the advisor can never separate himself or herself completely from the role of teacher—the one who evaluates performance (grading power) and has ultimate authority over the behavior of the student. He or she may put on the hat of "advisor" for a portion of a day but can never completely take off the hat of "teacher." Many feel this seriously handicaps the efforts of an advisor to assist advisees in dealing with personal, social, and moral issues that likely involve the home, their peers, or their teachers. This position has merit and could be a deciding factor in some school situations and cultures, but the pluses of merging teaming and advisory are many, and this option deserves serious consideration.

Who is in charge?

Any successful program requires ongoing support and oversight, and advisory is no exception. Indeed, the need for leadership is especially critical for advisory programs, as they are often launched amid some skepticism and doubt and always are initially viewed as being on probation.

In the 70s and 80s, advisory programs were usually labeled teacher-based guidance programs, and counselors who were professionally prepared as such were put in charge of developing the program with the assistance of a small committee of interested teachers. Counselors were also the most likely source of appropriate curriculum materials. Whether officially a part of a committee or not, the strong and active support of the principal is paramount to a program's success. This has been demonstrated to be the case time after time. An advisory program simply will not grow and flourish without the support of the lead administrator. But whoever is in charge, and however the leadership is distributed and organized, it is critical that the program has a "face and a personality."

The issues dealt with in the previous chapter are intertwined with the organizational matters dealt with in this chapter. Inevitably, organization and curriculum in advisory go hand in hand. Successful advisory programs simply can't be tight, independent entities—and they shouldn't be. In fact, only to the degree that the concept of advisory becomes inherent in the school's culture as well as in its curriculum will the relational work it seeks to do be fully effective.

5

Multiyear Advisory Groups

The life experience that has greatly informed my thinking was my first three years of teaching. I didn't get a math job my first year out, and I taught in a self-contained 6th grade classroom. And then the junior high was overcrowded, and I stayed with the same students for another year. We stayed together in 7th grade, and a few more kids joined us. And it was still overcrowded the next year, so we stayed together another year. So I taught the same students for three consecutive years. That experience has shaped my educational life—and so I am a firm believer in that kind of continuity. If teachers and students stay together by mutual consent for three years, you can do ever so much more than you can in one year. By the second year you can talk with kids about things that would be intrusive early in the first year when you're a stranger. It's an experience that's been extremely important. In fact, when I went into high school teaching, I insisted on teaching kids for more than one year. So there were lots of students whom I took right from geometry through their AP calculus, including one of my own daughters. This is where teachers get their renewal—from children they know well.

—Nel Noddings

When noted educational philosopher Nel Noddings describes her foundations in education, she uses the above story of de facto looping in her first years of teaching the middle grades (Halford, 1998, p. 1). Why? Through reflection, she recognized what became essential in her educational enterprise—caring—and how opportunities for expressing caring were multiplied and enriched in a learning community that stayed together three years. She came to know her students thoroughly as people by working with them over successive years.

Multiyear plans

In one and two room rural schools, looping and multigrade conditions automatically prevailed and were not viewed as educationally undesirable situations. Student's work was largely individualized and personalized, no "one lesson for all" was delivered, students often worked together in small groups, and they informally taught one another. Existing there and then was a situation that we would now label—with approval— as "a close learning community."

But time moved along, and as school systems in the states developed, with consolidation leading to the closing of most very small schools, these practices went by the board. The seemingly sensible and efficient graded school system quickly became standard, although, it should be noted, it was never promoted by educators as pedagogically the best way to provide an education. The resulting success of our nation in putting into place public schools that serve all American youth is an achievement of remarkable and historic proportions, and it was made possible in part by the uniform organizational plan imposed. And at that time educators were not as aware of the extent of individual differences as they soon came to be. But, it soon became apparent to many educators that something good from an educational standpoint had been lost in the march to install the graded school concept. This ladder concept that matched chronological age with specific levels of achievement just didn't match up to the realities of human growth and development. This first became quite apparent when the vast majority of the students retained in first grade for failing to learn how to read were boys.

At any rate, some practices from the one room school have continued to operate in small numbers. Looping, earlier usually labeled as student-teacher progression, has been practiced in a limited number of elementary schools across the decades, and the non-graded primary, advanced by John Goodlad and Robert Anderson (1959), was big in the 1950s and 60s. Now, in the middle school movement, multiyear strategies have been advanced as especially appropriate for young adolescents whose timetables of growth are so varied. Having the same professionals guiding the students' learning and development as they go through the changes associated with puberty just makes sense. Looping and multiage grouping both provide the desired long-term relationship and offer most of the same benefits, although each has a couple of distinct benefits—and a few perceived drawbacks.

Looping. By definition, looping involves a class or a team of students staying with the same teacher or team for two or more successive years. At the end of two or three years, the students move on to new teachers, and the looping teacher (or teachers) drops back to start with a new group of students. Nationally recognized educational leader Linda Darling-Hammond (1998) has stated:

> Research has found that students experience much greater success in schools structured to create close, sustained relationships among students and teachers. In high achieving countries like Japan, Germany, Sweden, and Switzerland, teachers often stay with the same students for two or more years and teach them more than one subject so that their teaching is informed by greater knowledge of the students and how they learn. Studies find that more ambitious learning goals can be tackled with greater success when students' and teachers' work is less fragmented and when time is available to support serious work. (p. 18)

An NMSA research summary on looping (Thompson, Frantz, and Miller, 2009) provides much the same support for this old practice that has experienced a comeback:

> The overall structure as well as academic and social support afforded to students and families involved in looping ought to lead to increased involvement and familiarity with school systems. Not only do students and families benefit from looping, teachers and administrators benefit as well. Teachers and administrators are better able to meet students and families where they are and propel them forward when capitalizing on knowledge of students' abilities. This in-depth knowledge is gained over time—a luxury of the looping classroom. The investment of time, cultivation of relationships, and prolonged engagement associated with looping promote an academic environment in which most people flourish. (p. 1)

Through the sequential exposure to young learners over multiple years, teachers develop the understandings and deeply grounded expertise needed to guide the developmental progression toward adolescence. They discover that the longer-term relationship supports the academic achievement and overall learning of students in ways previously unavailable.

Multiage grouping. The long-term student teacher relationship is also gained in a multiage grouping arrangement in which sixth, seventh, and eighth graders are enrolled in a team. During his time with the Alpha team at Vermont's Shelburne Middle School, Jim saw the power of multiage teaching firsthand. Observing the advantages for both students and teachers as they worked together over multiple years, he witnessed the expanded possibilities for learning that are unique to having a broad mix of ages present, including the effectiveness of students teaching one another.

Carol Smith, a veteran of Alpha's multiage setting, elaborated on an important phenomenon we call "leveling" that occurs in a multiage unit,

> Students of various ages have the opportunity to try on a variety of roles as they become ready to do so. Older students help younger students, and quite often, younger students emerge as leaders as well.

> Our team is family like, with oldest, youngest, and middle children all at the same time. For each child there is the chance to take on each of those roles and move out of his/her family designation. We believe this gives students a wider perspective of themselves and others, offering students greater chances to succeed in a wider variety of roles.

> Being the "youngest child" gives students permission to ask a lot of questions, rely on others, watch how others do things, try new things, make mistakes in a safe environment, and know there is time to try again.

> The "middle child" has the rare gift of time to practice. He/she knows the systems and procedures of the team....Being successful at some of the things that gave difficulty the year before is exhilarating and self-affirming.... Leadership opportunities present themselves when students are ready.

> As the "oldest" in their eighth grade year, students have now risen to the top of the three-year cycle and are the leaders they have learned how to be. This year offers many opportunities to work in partnership with the teachers, be role models for others. (George & Lounsbury, 2000, pp. 26–27)

Research on multiyear arrangements

Studies on multiyear grouping are, unfortunately, limited, and very few studies specifically deal with middle grades multiage grouping. Research is sparse, due in part to the fact that in multiage settings, it is difficult if not impossible to isolate the variable of multiage grouping and its effects from those of related instructional and environmental factors (Hoffman, 2003). The lack of apt quasi-experimental settings frustrates researchers. There are, however, many successful ongoing cases or examples where students' academic achievement and overall development both exceeded expectations. There is also considerable empirical evidence of how multiage groupings yield benefits in relationships and improved community interactions as well as in academic achievement. See Kuntz (2005), *The Story of Alpha: A Multiage, Student-Centered Team—33 Years and Counting* for the full story of this long-standing, highly successful program.

In a national study of 33 middle grades schools known to use some form of grouping that provided long-term, teacher-student relationships, 17 respondents reported utilizing multiage grouping while 11 reported using looping (George and Lounsbury, 2000). These schools reported that the long-term student-teacher relationships were instrumental in significant improvements in each of the following areas:

- Classroom climate

- Teacher advocacy for students

- Quality of instruction

- Student achievement

- Parental involvement

- Teacher-to-teacher relationships (pp. 96–100).

Multiyear advisories

The materials above that dealt with multiyear arrangements as a basis for conducting instruction have almost completely answered the question "What are the benefits of looping and multiage grouping for advisories?" Having advisees spend three years with the same advisor yields comparable benefits in the personal-social and academic development of students. Multiyear advisories were fairly common among pioneering middle schools in the 70s and 80s, although they never became widespread, as new middle schools put their priority on establishing the less adventuresome interdisciplinary teams. Now, however, there is a resurgence of interest in and development of both multiyear advisory programs and interdisciplinary teams.

A wise teacher observed, "You can talk about caring for students all you want. But all that caring doesn't amount to much if you don't know your students *really, really well*." Working with the same advisees for multiple years builds both strong relationships and the capacity for true caring. Also able to develop over time are deep teacher-to-student relationships that are important to building community. Finally, on the most practical level, no time is lost in getting acquainted when a new school year begins.

The Big Picture Learning Movement is an example of a major reform effort that gives advisory a prominent place in its program. The program was co-founded by Dennis Littky, the courageous organizing principal of Shoreham-Wading River Middle School that became the first real model of the middle school idea. Big Picture Schools have 10 distinguishing features including "one student at a time" and "advisory structure."

> The advisory structure is the core organizational and relational structure of a Big Picture school. It is the heart and soul of the school and is often described as the "home' and "second family" by students. (Big Picture Learning, 2008)

Each student in a Big Picture school is a part of a group of not more than fifteen students who work with the same advisor throughout their entire high school career.

Another example is provided by the Pacific Cascade Middle School cited earlier where a multigrade advisory group meets bi-weekly for half-hour classes called Lynx Life. In multigade classes of 25 students, students learn life skills not taught in core curriculum classes. The students forge a connection with their advisor whom they stay with for all three years of middle school and with their classmates from all three grade levels.

The seventh and eighth graders give the sixth graders strategies for staying organized and succeeding in middle school. Each advisory is assigned a color, and when the school had competitions, they are held by colors rather than by grade levels as in former years. Lynx Life has been an opportunity for the whole school to come together as a community.

Private schools and charter schools seem to be building advisory into their programs with some regularity. For instance, Wildwood, a private school previously cited in Chapter 2, has made advisory a distinguishing feature of its educational program. Students begin in the fifth grade and continue through high school with the same advisor. Another example is The University Preparatory Academy in Detroit, whose mission is to prove that urban children can succeed in college through providing personalized learning with relentless commitment, has a looped advisory program in which groups of 17 students stay together with an advisor. Students receive instruction in two of the core subjects from their advisor each year.

While our North American advisory status study lacked a specific inquiry about looped advisory, approximately 15 percent of the respondent schools indicated use of multiyear options for advisory. Since 2002, Highly Qualified Teacher (HQT) requirements of the No Child Left Behind Act (NCLB) have limited staffing options for both multigrade and looped instruction models. However, as far as advisory is concerned, neither multigrade nor looped formats for advisory are similarly limited. The main difficulty in instituting either of these formats often lies with the hesitancy of teachers to engage in a "different" approach. Once it is underway, however, its merits became obvious, and advisors provide valuable insights to the classroom teachers that pay off academically.

In a qualitative investigation of advisory programs, Sarah Brody Shulkind (2007) noted benefits of looped advisory on student achievement. She stated, "As an advisor following kids for two years, there was really a significant academic impact that went on … in terms of being able to follow up on kids, track their progress, and talk with their parents, and being someone who really knows how far you can push" (NASSP, 2008, p. 2).

The possibility of groups or individual relationships stagnating over several years and prolonging bad chemistry between certain advisors and advisees is sometimes a concern. However, if an advisory group is successful in carrying out its relational work, any bad chemistry in relationships would have been resolved through the dialogues and conferences that are a part of advisory. As to stagnation of relationships and the need to move people out of a group, teacher Carol Smith advised that after almost 30 years working with a multiage team, there were only a very small number of kids—perhaps a handful in each decade—who needed something else, and they helped them find it (Burns, 2007).

Entering sixth graders benefit from having the guidance of seventh and eighth graders without the usual taunting of freshmen. Multiage advisory integrates new students into the building quickly and efficiently; incoming sixth graders can be welcomed by their future advisory group before they come to the middle school, and during the first week each advisory student can make efforts to welcome the new sixth graders in their groups.

Additional benefits of three-year relationships include reducing inter-grade conflicts, establishing a family atmosphere, increasing the ease of younger students in asking directions and requesting help with their lockers, and making apparent to older students how much they have learned and grown. Teachers increase their awareness of developmental needs across the age span of middle grades and are more able to differentiate their academic coursework to meet students' needs.

Example: Multiage House. Back in the dark ages (1980) at Pueblo Junior High School where Jim was a young teacher, Assistant Principal Jud Mohart fulfilled the administrative need to occasionally bring students together at some point in the day by inventing "House," an alternative to daily homeroom. Mohart assigned groups of 20 to 24 randomly selected students from all three grade levels to each full-time faculty member.

House didn't meet everyday, only when needed. A House session could be 10, 15, 20, or more minutes depending on the task at hand. Although House most often took place at the end of the school day, it could happen at the start or in the middle of the day. Morhart, a scheduling master, could tweak any day's schedule, perfectly rationing needed minutes for House from the rest of the day's classes. Just as quickly, he could reprogram the bell schedule, and in a few more minutes he would deliver an aromatic ditto copy of the adjusted schedule to each teacher's mailbox.

House wasn't based on the typical teacher-student relationship. It provided time and a place where an adult and a group of emerging adolescents had an opportunity to be themselves and where achievement and grading weren't concerns. Even though the primary purpose of a day's meeting was routine, such as collecting interim grading reports or disseminating some important school-home communiqué, the social context was always relaxed. In spite of the indefinite nature of House with its usually short sessions, these casual interactions were valuable opportunities to establish a different kind of relationship between adult and youngster. It was there that Jim got to know Rachel, one of those atypical, typical young adolescents so interesting to teach.

> Rachel was 12 heading for 15 when I first met her, and she already really liked to dress the part. What part? You'd have to ask her. The costume du jour was a long winter scarf with a matching purple beret. That season the scarf and beret were her signature accessories. By ninth grade, punk was chic, and she donned a sleeveless denim jacket embroidered with scores of safety pins. Her most outlandish combination with that punked jacket was a pink chiffon tutu, black tights, and white high-top sneakers. She knew that particular outfit made me groan, but my opinion was irrelevant to her fashion choices.

House provided the unstructured time over three years to really get to know Rachel and the other students in advisory without the usual pressures of the student-teacher relationship.

While there are occasional recommendations for multiage academic teams in the professional literature, proposals to organize multiage advisories are more likely to be found. Why? Somehow, multiage advisory sounds doable while multiage teaching with the melding of various courses of study sounds like a more radical and insurmountable change. In fact it shouldn't be—we predict, as you might suspect, that multiage teaming will become more common in the years ahead as the many academic and other advantages of the long-term student teacher relationship become apparent to more and more middle level leaders.

Multiage advisory, while it may be fairly easy to inaugurate, still calls for extra effort to build support. Its effectiveness in dissolving the dissonance between grade levels and minimizing negative entitlements associated with being the upper classman makes it worth doing. Multiage advisory assuages differences and barriers based on grade levels and turns them into positive forces that support learning. It also provides a prime setting for discussing the many personal, social, and moral issues with which young adolescents wrestle.

A definitive finding in our 2008 study of advisory was that while up to four-fifths of respondent schools utilized single-grade groupings for advisory, a very interesting 13 percent reported using multiage advisories (Burns et al., 2009). By selecting this approach and dedicating the extra time and effort for these special cohorts, these schools could be classified as progressive middle schools.

This multiage approach requires specific effort by advisors each year as they integrate first-year students with the more experienced second- and third-year members. Much of this effort is "front loaded;" the critical work of this integration is focused during the first week each school year, an act of "breaking the ice." The older students are particularly good at orienting new members of the community. Experienced multiage advisors do say that their multiage groupings also require a certain amount of troubleshooting and on-the-spot maintenance during the year, but this is true in any advisory program. Reflecting upon his experience with the multiage House program, Jim recalled occasionally putting out brush fires between ninth grade teens and the younger tweens in seventh grade. What he emphasized, however, were the overwhelming opportunities a multiage grouping provides to get to know students well as persons and in a different way than in an academic context.

While there are reasons why some middle grade faculties may not be ready for multiage instruction, there are fewer limitations on organizing multiage advisory groups. The most important success factor, as is always the case, is faculty buy-in. Making multiage groups work with teachers and students used to single-grade settings or who are less than fully committed is a real challenge. It often helps to point out that any class of students in a middle school is, in fact, multiage. In a typical seventh grade class there will almost always be at least three years represented and sometimes even four. Different birthdays and perhaps the presence of repeaters or accelerated pupils make this condition normal. The assumptions we make about age and grades just don't hold up when checked. Do a run down in several of your classes and see if the generalization holds true

The many and obvious benefits of using either a looping or a multiage arrangement for structuring an advisory program warrant any school that is in the process of establishing an advisory program to give serious consideration to one of these arrangements that provide long-term relationships.

6

Nurturing, Assessing, and Evaluating Advisory

This we know to be true: Advisories that are unsuccessful, more often than not, are the result of inadequate initial preparation and insufficient ongoing nurturing. Our experiences working with advisory programs have made the importance of preparing advisors crystal clear. But even that is not enough!

No matter how carefully your program has been planned and how fully your advisors have been prepared, the program will not succeed unless the existing culture is ready or has been made ready to "take it in." The program has to be seen as aligning with and compatible with the values and beliefs that are inherent in that culture. Too often a pedagogically sound program has been planted in soil that simply wasn't able to offer the nurture needed to sustain it. Often a full year of consideration by the faculty and staff may be needed with ample opportunities for parents, the board of education, and others to be involved in various discussions—discussions that need to be more philosophical than managerial. Critical total faculty buy-in comes as the result of ample opportunities for everyone to think, read, and talk about advisory—and this takes time. Although an intellectual understanding and acceptance of advisory may come quickly, emotional acceptance evolves slowly.

Deconstructing myths about advisory

Efforts to institute advisory programs often meet with resistance because of an inadequate understanding of what this "new" educational idea is all about. The grapevine has perpetuated a number of false assumptions about advisory. Four of the most insidious myths follow and will be dealt with in turn.

Myth 1: To be a good advisor, you need the skills of a counselor.

Myth 2: Advisory requires advisors and advisees to become friends.

Myth 3: Running advisory requires an additional preparation.

Myth 4: Advisory is mainly for "at risk" students and can serve as group therapy.

1. To be a good advisor you need the skills of a counselor. Sounds logical, doesn't it? After all, doesn't being an advisor require shifting away from one's normal teacher role and taking on a different one? Not really. For some it may require moving a bit toward a more *affective* teacher role, but we see that as the relational aspect of teaching that all middle level teachers should be practicing.

Effective classroom management, is largely based upon rapport with students. That *rapport,* based on what Jacob Kounin (1970) called "with-it-ness," is based on really knowing one's students, expressing care about their interests and concerns, and acknowledging their voice. Admittedly, such a shift toward the affective may feel different at first. However, it calls for none of the specialized skills of a counselor or therapist. Based on our collective decades in middle level schools, we have concluded that the few teachers who find that they are incapable of the relational-based responsibilities of advisory are admitting that they are not really well-suited for teaching young adolescents in the first place.

2. Advisory requires advisors and advisees to become friends. An ultimate aim of advisory is creating a caring and comfortable culture within and among the group, and it is certainly true that to *care* requires getting to know one's advisees as distinctive individuals. However, it is neither required nor desirable to dash well-established adult-student boundaries. For example, knowing a student well enough to understand his or her passion for a hobby, music, or a pet does not require becoming either a best friend or a surrogate parent. In-depth knowledge about what motivates advisees enhances advisors' abilities to communicate with parents and to engage in three-way conversations about educational progress. Becoming a "best buddy" with a student would detract from conversations about progress and inhibit your effectiveness as an advisor. As you read and learn more about advisories, you will uncover cases where advisors and advisees did develop valued friendships. And frequently advisees will come back to visit advisors when they are in high school because a genuine relationship had been established.

3. Running advisory requires an additional preparation. Anything that prompts adaptive stress and initial discomfort comes hand-in-hand with teaching new or unfamiliar content. It comes, too, with establishing one's "chops" as an advisor, but as was noted earlier in the curriculum chapter, advisory is never didactic and you are seldom "on stage." The foreign or "uncomfortableness" aspect for some could be in turning the lead role over to the advisees once the ball is in the air. Advisors have to gracefully move between the roles of facilitator and co-participant. At first, you can expect to provide the topics, but as the group coalesces, students will bring their authentic topics to the table.

4. Advisory is mainly for "at risk" students and can serve as group therapy. This misconception may arise from leadership desperate for quick fixes for serious problems plaguing students. There are students who do need special services, counseling, therapeutic support groups, and support services such as those of a social worker—but advisory does not provide such services. Advisory is truly for everyone, and its attendant benefits, including enhanced school success, improved sense of well-being, and satisfaction with school, accrue to both learners and teachers (Felner, Jackson, Kasak, Mulhall, Brand & Flowers, 1997). Advisory is about developing natural, normal relationships. It should not be, whatsoever, about therapeutic intervention.

Giving prospective advisors the opportunity to air concerns such as those inherent in these myths and then confirming the true parameters of advisory is a good early step in preparing advisors for their new role. If possible, have an experienced advisor from a nearby school come and talk with the group. If that is not possible, you can bring in such voices of experience via the Internet.

Know thyself

One aspect of this preparation of advisees involves self-reflection—each individual examining honestly his or her personality, philosophy, disposition, and social skills as well as recalling his or her own experiences growing up. Because they are expected to get to know their advisees well, advisors need to let advisees know them as persons. Sharing some pictures, including one when you were 12 or 13, and personal stories from your adolescent years works wonders in building trust and establishing connections with advisees.

Another thing you can do is practice asking open questions that keep the conversation going, ones that can't be answered with a yes or no. For instance, "How would you feel about being involved in the seventh grade play?" rather than "Do you want to try out for the play?" Another technique that is useful in advisory is that of responding merely by reflecting on the advisee's thoughts and feelings, which encourages the advisee to say more. For instance, if the advisee says "I was mad when my mother wouldn't let me go to Katrina's house last night to study." You might simply say, "You felt awful." this would indicate you are a sympathetic listener ready to hear more of what is on this student's mind. And, of course, teachers all know about the value of "wait time." Silence is a great prod, particularly when the topic at hand relates to feelings rather than a right answer.

It is something of a challenge eliciting non-school-related information about students without appearing to be probing in areas that students may feel is none of your business. In an interesting case study, Brown and Anfara (2001) probed the fine line between addressing the needs of young adolescents to be nurtured and supported, while simultaneously respecting their ever growing desire for independence and autonomy. Six middle schools in the Greater New Orleans and Greater Philadelphia Region were the study sites. At each site students and teachers with diverse opinions and experiences were interviewed. Brown and Anfara researched these key questions:

> Where does the line of student mingling end and teacher meddling begin? When does teacher prodding violate a student's right to privacy? What if students are uncomfortable with sharing and feel as though their personal lives are being invaded? How do teachers know where to draw the line between being interested and supportive and being nosy and interfering…
> (p. 17)

Some teachers in this study shared their frustrations:

> "The most negative aspect of the program was that students were reluctant to share."

> "Some faculty complained about students being committed to not sharing their thoughts and feelings on different issues discussed.

> "Their advisory groups were not interested in the list of subjects requested to be discussed and some of them maintained that there was a lack of student interest in the advisory group." (p. 17)

Here are some voices of the students in the study as they describe "teacher meddling.'"

> "Like some things I like about it [the advisory program] and some things I dislike— like having to tell them what I'm thinking or feeling about things—that's my business, not theirs. It's just okay."

> "We talk some, but not really cause that don't concern us. We don't want to talk about our problems with her. That's like taking time away from us. We want to be by ourselves."

> "So we don't really communicate with our teachers in guidance or advisory. They try to ask us personal questions like stuff about our families and stuff. I don't want them knowing any of that. Why they got to keep at it?" (p. 18)

Many students, of course, were keenly aware and appreciative of the attention given to them in advisory, as reflected in these comments:

> "I like it cause she [advisor] would talk to me about doing better. I got better in, like my behavior and um ... yeah, I am much better now."

> "Like, um, cause last year I had a bad year and like Mr. M. was my adopted buddy, or advisor, and if I got problems, I go to him."

> "Mr. J., cause like, he's helped me...I'm calming down and learning more stuff, like how to keep up with my work and everything."

> "Well, like she's [my advisor] the main one who always puts pressure on me so I could do better and stuff. So, it's like, she's my main teacher who gives me the most attention."

"Well, on the upside, since you're in a smaller group, you get to have more attention in each class. And in our classes of I believe there's 26 to 27 kids this year. So, that's a lot of kids to pay attention to. When there's 13 to 14 kids, you can be more alert and you can have more attention." (p. 22)

Teachers in this study offered interesting views on advisory, such as the following:

" I found that with the kids there was always a feeling like the kids in school were kind of out of control and now it seems like the energy is really generated towards this program and the kids seem to be more focused all around, academically and socially. I think I found the advisory program made a big difference."

"It was a way for me to connect with her [my advisee]. I sat on her a little bit and she told me she felt it made a big difference. She became more organized because there was somebody watching over her shoulder, checking up to see that things were being done."

"It gives you a different feeling about your relationships that you should have. In a big city like this, students could get lost. It's a big system too."

"I like the individual attention that we can give them. One boy I was working with, um, he was basically failing when we started. We continually worked, and worked, and worked.... His attitude has been definitely positive and he is doing his homework and he's made a 100% turnaround. I'm just keeping my fingers crossed that it continues."

Brown and Anfara point out "An important word that seems to have gotten misplaced in some advisory programs is *respectful*. The study data revealed that teachers need to be sensitive to and respectful of their students' right to privacy. One teacher reported that the fine line between mingling and meddling was the basis for lively discussions among the faculty. "While the faculty got into some heated debate about the fine line, it did give us an opportunity to confront some issues and discuss the real purpose of the advisory program at our school."

It is obvious that a first priority for advisors is to establish meaningful relationships with advisees, and this needs to be done slowly but continuously in ways that are compatible with your personality and style. It is not a matter of following certain steps; it is rather something that has to evolve from your being, your disposition, and your unique personhood—from someone who knows himself or herself well.

Gathering baseline data

Another task that must be attended to early on is the gathering of baseline data. Facts and figures that reflect existing conditions need to be recorded to have a basis later on for determining whether the program has made a difference. For instance, how will the absentee rate now compare with the rate after the program has been in operation for a year? Other facts and figures to gather include in-school suspension rates, the extent of bullying and fights reported, standardized test scores, grades earned by students, number of parent contacts, extent of participation in school activities, and results of any surveys or questionnaires given. While subjective data such as opinions expressed by the students themselves, their parents, or by the advisors are valuable, nothing impresses others quite like being able to cite specific figures and numbers.

In addition, some "softer" data sources should be set aside. These could include copies of annual or periodic reports prepared for accreditation, strategic planning documents, and reports relating to accreditation by state or regional associations. Gather as much documentation as possible to draw upon when you later try to determine the program's impact by examining the "then" and the "now."

It is important to have made clear to all parties from the beginning that those traits, behaviors, and dispositions advisory seeks to develop are not easily measured or acquired quickly. To expect measurable changes in an inaugural year is unwise. Subjective data in the form of opinions and reflections from those parties involved, such as are suggested below, may comprise early evaluations.

Evaluating and improving advisory

To best respond to concerns that arise after advisory is underway, keep advisory as a lead item on the agendas for all meetings—team meetings, committee meetings, parent-community meetings, and faculty meetings. This allows you to address important problems and share successes as they arise.

To provide needed professional development experiences, tap into those information sources available to determine what in the program is working and what is not. Envision one full year of advisory as the first *complete cycle*—whether thinking in terms of systems theory or action research—and ascertain facts and stories to develop a portrait of what is happening in advisory, and most important, how the participants themselves are viewing it.

Unfortunately, this important process of planned program assessment has often been absent from advisory programs. The reasons? Perhaps in this era of intense accountability, it is assessment fatigue. Perhaps advisory coordinators are wary of asking teachers to do one more assessment. Perhaps it's fear of negative responses. As a result, teacher-advisors seldom obtain any organized feedback about how they are doing as advisors. As a result, they never hear how they are doing, even when they are doing excellent, creative work! Receiving no feedback on whether things are working as planned and whether they are succeeding in developing relationships built on trust leaves one message: "In the big picture, advisory is just not very important." In such situations, even well-designed programs quickly begin to stagnate.

Survey instruments

What we offer here are three starter tools for help in answering the fundamental question "How is advisory doing?" These instruments simply solicit the views of advisees, advisors, and observers. If you obtain these formal data even once during the first year or, from the advisors and advisees, at several intervals, you will have evaluation information that is sufficiently rich to make adjustments and revisions. Add items or questions to these instruments to fit your situation.

Student survey instrument. This first tool is designed to be completed by the advisees at least once during their first year in the middle school—usually grade six. Rather than going immediately to direct inquiry about advisory, the instrument intentionally begins with seven items that solicit their perspectives about the overall school experience before honing in on four advisory items. Notice, too, that it is labeled as a student survey, not just an advisee survey. The data gathered from these first questions are of real value, although they are not directly related to the advisory program.

Figure 6.1

Student Survey

Please answer these questions about your experience this year.

1. What was your favorite class? _____

   _____

2. What about the class made it best for you? _____

   _____

3. Who are your two (or more) best friends in school? _____

   _____

4. How long have you known them? Were they your friends before coming to this school? _____

   _____

5. What is your least favorite thing about school? In a few words, explain why you dislike it. _____

   _____

6. What sports do you enjoy? Are you a member of any team?

   _____

7. To what student organizations/clubs do you belong?

   _____

8. Rate your experience with advisory.

	strongly agree				strongly disagree
Fun activities	5	4	3	2	1
Good source of information	5	4	3	2	1
Helped me understand middle school	5	4	3	2	1
Helped with school work	5	4	3	2	1
Got to know my teacher(s) better	5	4	3	2	1
Helped develop new friendships	5	4	3	2	1
Helped resolve conflicts	5	4	3	2	1

9. Tell us in your own words what your favorite part of advisory was.

   _____

   _____

10. Tell us in your own words what your least favorite part of advisory was.

    _____

    _____

In this format, short-answer qualitative responses are combined with very quick response-scale checkoffs. This makes the data easy to tally and sort. Since compiling and comparing the open-ended responses takes some time, we suggest initial review and summary of these data be done by the advisors who will only have 10-15 respondents to summarize. As you know, personally worded responses tend to be more meaningful, so you should give due consideration to asking students to sign their names. The information will be more candid and accurate when a response is anonymous. A good alternative to asking for the student's name is to have the student indicate only the name of his/her advisor, so data can be disaggregated to specific advisory and grade level groups. After the "thank you" at the end, you can allow students to add their name if they would like to follow up and discuss their answers with someone.

Assessments of advisory should be ongoing. Modify the survey appropriately and use it periodically The major evaluation at the final year of your three-year trial run should, of course, ask a number of culminating questions about the advisory experience as a whole and involve some interviews and other means of taking stock.

Teacher assessment of advisory. To get the views of advisors, we recommend for starters the simple "yes/no" style checklist like the sample shown in Figure 6.2. For comprehensive evaluation and reliability, retain a common core of about ten questions to be used each time the survey is administered. Beyond that retained core, however, improvise. Add several questions pertinent to current trends, conditions, or modifications in the program, such as suggested by items 9 and 10 in Figure 6.2.

Figure 6.2

Advisor Checklist for Assessing the Advisory Program

1. The aims of advisory are posted in my advisory area.   Y   N

2. I understand and use these goals and objectives in selecting advisory activities.
                                                                                       Y   N

3. My advisees support and can explain the program in terms of its purposes.
                                                                                       Y   N

4. Each of my advisees has daily contact with me and knows how to connect with me outside of advisory times.   Y   N

5. I have an advisory partner to turn to when I need assistance, such as with a larger group activity.   Y   N

[and so on . . .]

9. I have found extended advisory on Mondays and Wednesdays to be useful.
                                                                                       Y   N

10. I have found the shorter advisory period on Friday to be helpful.
                                                                                       Y   N

This type of survey is quick and easy to administer, tabulate, and share results. The satisfaction/dissatisfaction scale collects feedback (data) that advisors can immediately use as they reflect on how they are doing in advisory as a whole. This fast survey can be administered several times throughout the year. From a leadership perspective, taking the seven or so minutes necessary to use it at the lead of a faculty meeting (during alternate months) sends the following important messages: we care about the advisory program; we care how advisory is going for you; and we are using your input to make changes. Doing this also reminds everyone to reflect upon and attend to the relational work of teaching.

An assessment sharing session

At some point you may want to consider holding an assessment sharing session where advisors voluntarily present findings and observations from their groups. This type of informal collaborative reporting (a common action research tool) is not only surprisingly informative, but also advisors find it an entertaining and satisfying means of celebrating successes and commiserating over shared failures.

An important role for the advisory coordinator in moderating such a sharing session is managing the sequence of presentations. This isn't difficult. Those with positive outcomes will naturally rise to share first. This is where the able coordinator uses his or her insider knowledge to ensure that several of the best, most compelling stories—or as John Van Maanen (1988) calls them, "tales of the field"—are reserved for last, to uplift after those with more complaints than praise have had their say.

Assessing teachers as advisors

At the outset, we need to say that the use of this tool is controversial. Whether you use it will depend largely on your response to this question. "Is teacher evaluation in your school experienced collectively as a positive process that focuses on improving teaching and student learning, or is it conceived as an adversarial, administrative function?"

To the extent that performance evaluation is perceived positively—that professional growth is supported through focused professional development and through what Roland Barth (1991) calls "colleagueship"—educators will have few problems with incorporating advisory as one part of the established plan for professional growth. Without the aforementioned environment of trust, we advise school leaders to tread very carefully before adding advisory into the evaluation process. Fundamental problems with supervision and evaluation will need to be fixed first.

Much of this harkens back to the Golden Rule, to "do unto others as you would have them do unto you." It begins with school leaders, whether principals or coordinators, taking a very active role in advisory by modeling and verbally supporting positive actions. Too often, educators have become turned off to evaluation and assessment because it has been "done unto them;" that is, something imposed. The entire process of evaluation, as we see it, is a process that is collective, collaborative, and formative. It is *collective* in that it secures the results of everyone observing and sharing. It is *collaborative* in that successes and struggles are shared continuously, making it more rewarding for everyone. Finally, it is useful and informative to the individual, ensuring that it is a *formative*, nothing like external "done unto" summative judgments associated with accountability systems.

Assuming that the school's leaders are fully on board with advisory—and the emotional climate is reasonably favorable, we suggest the following unfinished observation tool be revised and expanded and then used by a mentor, a colleague, or a supervisor. The advisor himself or herself might use it to capture information while an advisory session is underway.

Figure 6.3

Assessing the Advisory Program - Observation Form

1. The advisor has prominently posted the grade-level aims for advisory.

   Y   N

2. Advisory is at an appropriate time of day for the observed activity.

   Y   N

3. The advisory activity seemed appropriate for the interests and maturity of the students.   Y   N

4. The number of students in this group is appropriate for the activity.

   Y   N

5. The advisor appeared actively and positively engaged in the activity, but did not dominate.   Y   N

6. . . . .   Y   N

A formal assessment can help improve and reinvigorate advisory, and much is lost when a carefully conducted evaluation is overlooked. If advisory isn't assessed objectively and critically, problems and aggravations will build, important successes will fail to be recognized, and the advisory program will be judged only by informal comments made in the teachers' lounge. Since advisory is so much about educators and students knowing and caring for one another in new and meaningful ways, *voice* and being heard are fundamental to the process. The assessments we describe are all about hearing participants' voices. If leaders don't solicit such, only the complaints are heard.

The only downside to evaluation efforts comes up in settings where the evaluation process has been abused to "get at" teachers, where assessment has been done unto them. In such settings, where the teachers are unhappy, advisory isn't likely to help too much. Finally, we would remind people of this famous principle uttered by Neila Connors (2000): "If you don't feed the teachers, they eat the students!"

Resource materials

To support and nurture an advisory program, particularly one that is just getting started, it is important to assemble a supply of relevant professional materials. Your existing professional shelf in the media center may include some books that have advisory in their contents, but you will likely need to purchase some newer materials. NMSA (now, AMLE) has published the following books dealing with advisory:

1. *Treasure Chest: A Teacher Advisory Source Book.* This perennial best seller includes 120 classroom-ready activities organized by topics.

2. *Treasure Chest II: Problem Solving Activities, Brain Stretchers, and Active Games* was published in 2009 to meet the demand for more such practical materials.

3. *Minds and Motion: Active Learning for the Creative Classroom.* Just released, this little book provides energizing activities that can be done in 15-20 minutes.

4. *Launching a Successful Advisory Program.* A Professional Development Kit. Use this kit with the entire faculty to ensure a successful program.

5. *Teaming and Advisory: Perfect Partners* presents a model that will revitalize your advisory program while strengthening your team.

6. *From Advisory to Advocacy: Meeting Every Student's Needs* provides a compelling rationale for student advocacy, details its implications and challenges, and provides specific activities.

7. *Advisory: Definitions, Descriptions, Decisions, Directions* assists faculties in reaching consensus about the right program for their schools.

8. *Goal Setting for Success*, a teacher handbook and a package of student notebooks, shows teachers and students how to set, monitor, and follow through on goals.

Having resources readily available to put in advisors' hands does a lot to quell understandable fears and uncertainties when a program is launched. Advisors should have some regular time set aside to compare notes and review resources. Supporting an advisory program has to be an ongoing affair.

7

It's About Time

You have now reached the last chapter of this book. As you journeyed through the chapters, we hope many ideas resonated with you and that you identified the approaches and proposals that would be right for your middle school. While every middle school should have an advisory program, implementation, unfortunately, has occurred slowly. Strangely, some educators still treat advisory as a possible add-on to a school's program, just something to consider later in the school's evolution. They miss the message that advisory is an essential element of a true middle school, a basic part of that sound, research-based and time-proven middle school concept. We hope the book will assist you and your school in taking that long-overdue step to establish an advisory program or to revitalize one that has flagged.

The work of middle grades educators is particularly critical because during this dynamic period of early adolescence, young people make decisions that will greatly impact their behavior as adults. This work is fundamentally relational work. Sound relationships are essential to engaging young adolescents in meaningful lessons and projects, and a well-established advisory program is a particularly powerful vehicle to strengthen that relational work of middle schools. Engage your school in an action research project as you lead in meeting the challenges of the 21st century.

We cannot afford to lose one student between the ages of ten and fifteen to a less-than-fulfilling life. If we lose them during these developmental years—education's second chance—we will never have a third chance. "Middle grade schools…are potentially society's most powerful force to recapture millions of youth adrift and help every young person thrive during early adolescence" (Carnegie Council on Adolescent Development, 1989).

The theme song from the movie *Crazy Heart* has a line that resonates here: "This ain't no place for the weary kind." Genuine developmentally responsive middle schools are staffed by educators who enthusiastically engage themselves in strong relational work through solid advisory programs that have a place for the weary kind and ways to invigorate them. When we make operational advisory programs in all our middle level schools, we can, as we did in the opening verse, claim genuinely that: "We're for young adolescents."

As you work to initiate a program, be aware of some developments or trends that will affect advisory in the years just ahead. Earlier we made the point that smaller is better. This is a research-supported generalization that has led to the creation of small schools, schools-within-a-school, and smaller teams. Two-person or partner teams are catching on in middle schools as is looping. Consider then this eventuality: two sixth grade teachers are responsible for the learning of 48 students for the bulk of the day. They also continue teaching these students as seventh graders, so they will come to know this limited number of individuals very, very well as they work with them in the block of time equivalent to four or five periods. As they follow an integrated curriculum approach and operate a student-centered classroom with the students actively involved in planning what and how they will study and learn, the concerns and needs of young adolescents in the personal-social realm will be dealt with as parts of the ongoing, problem-solving curriculum. In such a situation, a period and time set aside for advisory would be artificial and unnecessary.

Then consider another development that will impact advisory. All students, not just special education students, are now beginning to use individualized learning plans (IEPs). The movement to have students assume greater responsibility and personalize and individualize their education led to the development of journals and student-led conferences. The use of IEPs is an obvious next step. Many private and public schools have adopted such individualized programs. Although not identified as an IEP, students in the Alpha Team in Shelburne, VT, cited in Chapter 3, have for more than 35 years planned their own educational program. Two recent examples are The Big Picture Schools, cited in Chapter 5, and Linwood Middle School in North Brunswick, NJ, where students chart their own academic path with personalized student learning plans that include information about their learning styles, interests, career goals, and activities. An IEP, actually an electronic portfolio, goes with the student as he or she moves up the ladder. An advisor manages and monitors the individual's plan and remains with that student until graduation (Hu, 2010).

While middle schools will continue to fulfill their advisory responsibility as they must, the specific structures and ways schools use to meet that obligation will continue to evolve into practices not now common. Exactly how? As always, it all depends…

References

Alexander, W. M., & McEwin, C. K. (1989). *Schools in the middle: Status and progress.* Columbus, OH: National Middle School Association.

Ballard, E. (2003). *The bracelet*. Layton, Utah: Gibbs Smith.

Barth, R. (1991). *Improving schools from within*. New York: John Wiley & Sons, Inc.

Big Picture Learning. (2008). Advisory structures. Retrieved from http://www.bigpicture.org/2008/10/advisory-structure/

Brown, K. M., & Anfara, Jr., V. A. (2001). Competing perspectives on advisory programs: Mingling or meddling in middle schools. *Research in Middle Level Education Annual, 24*, 1-30.

Burkhardt, R., & Kane, J.T. (2005). An adult advocate for every student. In T. Erb (Ed.), *This we believe in action: Implementing successful middle schools* (pp. 63-76). Westerville, OH: National Middle School Association.

Burns, J. (2007). *The relational work of middle grades teachers: From advisory to relational dispositions*. (Doctoral dissertation, The University of Vermont). Retrieved from http://immerman.com/Documents/Burns%20Advisory.pdf

Burns, J., Behre Jenkins, J., Kane, T., Tenorio, M., & Maestas, D. (2009). North American middle grades advisories and related relational work. *Kokopelli Review, 1*(1). Retrieved from http://immerman.com/Documents/NMMLE%20Advisory.pdf

Burton, B. (2008). Acting against bullying in schools. In K. Donelan & A. O'Brien (Eds.), *The arts and youth at risk: Global and local challenges*. Cambridge, UK: Cambridge Scholars Press.

Carnegie Council on Adolescent Development. (1989). *Turning points: Preparing American youth for the 21st century*. New York: Carnegie Corporation.

Connors, N. (2000). *If you don't feed the teachers they eat the students!* Nashville, TN: Incentive Publications.

Connors, N. (1992). Teacher advisory: The fourth R. In Irvin, J. (Ed.), *Transforming middle level education: Perspectives and possibilities*. Boston: Allyn and Bacon.

Cross, D., Shaw, T., Hearn, L., Epstein, M., Monks, H., Lester, L., & Thomas, L. (2009). *Australian covert bullying prevalence study*. Perth, WA, Australia: Child Health Promotion Research Centre, Edith Cowan University.

Darling-Hammond, L. (1998). Alternatives to grade retention. *School Administrator, 55*(7), 18- 21.

Education World. (2004). Advice about middle school advisories. Retrieved from http://www.educationworld.com/a_curr/curr127.shtml

Erb, T. (Ed.). (2005). *This we believe in action: Implementing successful middle schools*. Westerville, OH: National Middle School Association.

Eyers, V., Cormack, P., & Barratt, R. (1992). *Report of the junior secondary review: The education of young adolescents*. Adelaide, SA, Australia: Department of Education and Children's Services.

Felner, R. D., Jackson, A. W., Kasak, D., Mulhall, P., Brand, S., & Flowers, N. (1997). The impact of school reform for the middle years: Longitudinal study of a network engaged in Turning Points-based comprehensive school transformation. *Phi Delta Kappan, 78*(7), 528-532, 541-550.

Galassi, J. P., Gulledge, S. A., & Cox, N. D. (1998). *Advisory: Definitions, descriptions,decisions, directions*. Columbus, OH: National Middle School Association.

Garvin, J. P. (1987). What do parents expect from middle level schools? *Middle School Journal, 18*(2), 3-4.

George, P. S., & Lounsbury, J. H. (2000). *Making big schools feel small: Multiage grouping, looping, and schools-within-a-school*. Westerville, OH: National Middle School Association.

Goodlad, J., & Anderson, R. (1959). *The non-graded elementary school*. New York: Teachers College Press.

Halford, J.M., (1998-1999). Longing for the sacred in schools: A conversation with Nel Noddings. *Educational Leadership, 56*(4), 28-32.

Hoffman, J. (2003). Multiage teachers' beliefs and practices. *Journal of Research in Childhood Education, 18*(1), 5–17.

Hoversten, C., Doda, N., & Lounsbury, J. (1991). *Treasure chest: A teacher advisory source book*. Columbus, OH: National Middle School Association.

Hu, W. (2010). In middle school, charting their course to college and beyond. Retrieved from http://www.nytimes.com/2010/03/01/education/01schools.html

Jackson, A. W., & Davis, G. A. (2000). *Turning points 2000: Educating adolescents in the 21st century*. New York: Teachers College Press.

James, M., & Spradling, N. (2002). *Advisory to advocacy: Meeting every student's needs*. Columbus, OH: National Middle School Association.

Kounin, J. S. (1970). *Discipline and group management in classrooms*. Huntington, NY: R. E. Krieger.

Kuntz, S. (2005). *The story of Alpha: A multiage, student-centered team—33 years and counting*. Westerville, OH: National Middle School Association.

Langford International (2009). *Quality Learning Tools*. Retrieved from http://www.langfordlearning.com/4day.htm

Lipka, R. (1997). Enhancing self-concept/self-esteem in young adolescents. In Irvin, J. (Ed.) *What research says to the middle level practitioner*. Columbus, OH: National Middle School Association.

Lorimer, M. (2006, February). Bullying. *NMSA Research summary*. Retrieved from http://www.nmsa.org/Research/ResearchSummaries/Bullying/tabid/709/Default.aspx

McEwin, C. & Alexander, W. (1988). *.Preparing to teach at the middle level*. Columbus, OH: National Middle School Association.

McEwin, C. K., Dickinson, T. S., & Jenkins, D. (1995). *America's middle schools: Practices and progress—A 25 year perspective*. Columbus, OH: National Middle School Association.

McEwin, C. K., Dickinson, T. S., & Jenkins, D. (2003). *America's middle schools in the new century: Status and progress*. Westerville, OH: National Middle School Association.

McEwin, C. K. & Greene, M. (2010). Results and recommendations from the 2009 national surveys of randomly selected and highly successful middle level schools. *Middle School Journal, 42*(1) 49-63.

MindMatters Technologies, Inc. (2009). Internet home page. Retrieved from: http://www.us-mindmatters.com/

Mizer, J. (1964). Cipher in the snow. *NEA Journal, 50*, 8-10.

National Association of Secondary School Principals. (2006). *Breaking ranks in the middle: Strategies for leading middle level reform*. Reston, VA: Author.

National Middle School Association. (1982). *This we believe*. Columbus, Ohio: Author.

National Middle School Association. (1995). *This we believe: Developmentally responsive middle level schools*. Columbus, Ohio: Author.

National Middle School Association. (2003). *This we believe: Successful schools for young adolescents*. Westerville, Ohio: Author.

National Middle School Association. (2010). *This we believe: Keys to educating young adolescents*. Westerville, Ohio: Author.

No Child Left Behind Act of 2001, 20 U.S.C. § 6319 (2008).

Noddings, N. (2005). Caring in education. *The encyclopedia of informal education*. Retrieved from www.infed.org/biblio/noddings_caring_in_education.htm

O'Toole, J., & Burton, B. (2009). *Acting against bullying: Using drama and peer teaching to reduce bullying*. Retrieved from http://www.education.com/reference/article/act-against-reduce-bullying-peer-teaching/

Putbrese, L. (1989). Advisory programs at the middle level: The students' response. *NASSP Bulletin, 73*(514), 111-115.

Queensland Government, Department of Education and Training (2002). *Social outcomes survey.* Brisbane, Qld, Australia: Author.

Rottier, J. (2001). *Implementing and improving teaming: A handbook for middle level leaders*. Westerville, OH: National Middle School Association.

Rottier, J., Woulf, T., Bonetti, D., & Meyer, E. (2009). *Teaming & advisory: Perfect partners*. Westerville, OH: National Middle School Association.

Seaford 6-12 School (2008). *Annual report*. Seaford, SA, Australia: Author.

Selby, M. (1997). She's no one's girl. *My dad is a superintendent*. Nashville, TN: MDM Records.

Senge, P. (1994). *The fifth discipline: The art and practice of the learning organization*. New York: Doubleday.

Sergiovanni, T. (2006). *Rethinking leadership: A collection of articles.* (2nd ed.). Thousand Oaks, CA: Corwin.

Shulkind, S. B. (2007). *Fostering connectedness through middle school advisory programs* (Doctoral dissertation, University of California Los Angeles). Retrieved from www.nassp.org/dissertation

Shulkind, S. B. (2008). *The power of advisories.* Podcast. Retrieved from http://www.nassp.org/ knowledge-center/school-leaders-review-podcasts

Shulkind, S. B., & Foote, J. (2009). Creating a culture of connectedness through middle school advisory programs. *Middle School Journal, 41*(1), 20-27.

Spear, R. (2005). Taking the lead in implementing and improving advisory. Westerville, OH: National Middle School Association.

Stevenson, C. (2002). *Teaching ten to fourteen year olds.* (3rd ed.). Boston, MA: Pearson.

Thompson, N. L., Franz, D. P., & Miller, N. (2009). Research summary: Looping. Retrieved from http://www.nmsa.org/Research/ResearchSummaries/Looping/tabid/2090/Default.aspx

Van Maanen, J. (1988). *Tales of the field: On writing ethnography.* Chicago, IL: University of Chicago Press.

Wildwood School. (2011). Meet Joel Murillo. Retrieved from http://www.wildwood.org/page.cfm?p=444

Yarrow, P. (2010). *Don't laugh at me: Teachers guide.* Retrieved from http://www.operationrespect. org/pdf/guide2.pdf

About the Authors

Dr. Jim Burns is a Chair of the Educational Leadership Department at New Mexico Highlands University. Jim is a director of the New Mexico Middle Level Educators Association and is the former Director of Member and Affiliate Services of National Middle School Association. He has an extensive background as a classroom teacher in middle grades and special education.

Jaynellen Behre *Jenkins* is currently the Principal of Woodside School in River Vale, NJ, and is a Past-President of the New Jersey Middle School Association. She has appeared on the Rachel Ray television program as an educational consultant. A consultant to the New Jersey Department of Education, Jaynellen has also been a creative middle grades teacher and administrator.

J. Thomas Kane is a retired middle school principal and now a consultant specializing in middle school education. Tom is a past-president of the New York State Middle School Association as well as a past-president of the New Jersey Middle School Association. He is currently a member of the AMLE Publications Review Committee and a Co-Facilitator of ASCD's Middle Grades Network. Tom has been a middle grades teacher, guidance counselor, and administrator as well as a substance abuse counselor and crisis intervention counselor at Covenant House in New York City.

CPSIA information can be obtained
at www.ICGtesting.com
Printed in the USA
FFOW05n2333050716